JESUS...
OR MONEY

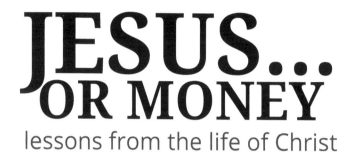

JESUS...
OR MONEY
lessons from the life of Christ

PARKS BROWN

This book is dedicated to all believers courageous enough to take a deeper and more challenging look at money and the role it plays in their lives by allowing God to speak to them through the teachings of His Son, Jesus Christ.

May His will be done in and through His people.

If any of you lacks wisdom, you should ask God, who gives generously to all without finding fault, and it will be given to you. But when you ask, you must believe and not doubt, because the one who doubts is like a wave of the sea, blown and tossed by the wind. That person should not expect to receive anything from the Lord. Such a person is double-minded and unstable in all they do. – James 1: 5–8

Trust in the Lord with all your heart and lean not on your own understanding. – Proverbs 3:5

Do not be wise in your own eyes: Fear the Lord and shun evil. – Proverbs 3: 7

CONTENTS

FOREWORD

This is a book written for Christians and therefore makes certain assumptions about the reader. The book includes several stories in the Bible and the words of Jesus where scriptural references are provided. In some cases of ideology, it is assumed the reader understands and agrees. For starters, we serve a jealous God. By this, I mean He demands our love, faith, trust and devotion to Him above all and everything else. The Ten Commandments in the Old Testament and Jesus' words in the New Testament remind us that first and foremost we are to love the Lord our God and have no other gods before Him.

Christ's ministry and teachings centered on faith in God and faith in him as the Son of God. Jesus repeatedly reminded, chastised and rebuked his disciples and followers for having little faith. He declared that with faith all things were possible. He continually emphasized that our trust and belief in Him was a cornerstone for living a victorious Christian life and essential in getting to heaven.

A belief that Jesus is the Son of God is the basis of our salvation. Faith in Christ and belief in what he said is at the heart of the Christian life. In turn, Jesus used real time examples and parables to teach and show His followers where their faith, lives and hearts were focused. Jesus reminded us how things of this world can deter and deceive us from a pure unadulterated faith in Him and Him alone.

FOREWORD

This book is about faith, trust and our hearts. Christ demanded faith in Him and Him alone. Our faith must be in Jesus and nothing else. A faith that relies on Jesus AND something else is not faith in Him alone. A faith in Jesus OR something else, is a choice that leads to death and destruction.

Jesus used parables and examples to show men where they put faith in Him OR other things of this world. In issues that were deep rooted in the heart of men, Christ would use decisions men made, parables and circumstances to show their faith was in God OR something else. This book focuses on one such object, money. This book focuses on an object that can be a distraction and serve as a means to put our faith and trust in something other than our heavenly father. This book shows where money has been and can be the object of men's faith and trust.

Many of the parables, words and stories involving Christ' teaching about money show that money is a powerful master. Christ reminds us that money can cause us to make a choice of following Jesus OR money. The examples used in this book show where the disciples and everyday people made decisions of having faith in Jesus OR money. Are we so different today?

It is easy to read the Bible, use scriptural commentary, study notes provided in the margin or sermons we have heard to see where people thousands of years ago were deceived and sidetracked by money. Stories from the Bible can encourage us and haunt us when it comes to what Christ said about money. Jesus focused on how we use money and how it reveals our hearts and faith.

The question is, do we stop and see ourselves and how we deal with money in these Biblical stories? Do we see the parallels between them and us; then and now? Is the Word alive and convicting in your life regarding money? Is the Word just an old book with stories of people you don't relate to? Is there anything new the Holy Spirit wants to reveal to you regarding your faith, your heart and money??

While you read this book, ask yourself if it is possible that YOU are the same as the characters in the stories. Where do you make the decision between faith in Jesus OR money. Let me warn you ahead of time, you can not determine this on your own. Let me also warn you, the names and stories used may not be people you want to relate to. The people in Christ's' day couldn't see without him digging into them and revealing their hearts. You will not be able to unless you proceed with an open, repentant and teachable mind as well.

Before you proceed, spend a few minutes in prayer asking the Holy Spirit to forgive you for any and all times that you have put money ahead of Him....the times you do it consciously and unconsciously. Ask Him to reveal your heart and show you His. Consider reading the book with a friend to bounce questions off each other.

Money is so essential to our lives. It can be a blessing and it can be a curse depending on the condition of your heart. It can come from God, and it can come from Satan. It can be used to glorify the Kingdom and it can be used to glorify our selves. It does reveal our hearts and where we put our faith, but you have to be willing to dive DEEP and allow the Spirit to show you, don't rely on your own understanding.

The question to ask with every page, every story and every day of our lives, is...do we want and need Jesus and Jesus alone? Is Jesus alone the center of our faith and trust? Does the way we handle, pursue and deal with money show we have faith in Jesus AND our money? If that's the case, then our faith may be in Jesus OR money.

ACKNOWLEDGMENTS

First and foremost to my wife and helpmate, Joy, for her unwavering love, encouragement, and support of this work—and of my entire life. She is a gift from God that I treasure.

My sincere gratitude to my sister-in-Christ, Lindsay Baker, for her expertise, talents, friendship, and willingness to consistently model the living Christ year after year.

A special thanks to Jim Kelly and Ed Cain for their input and support, without which this endeavor would not be possible.

And a special thanks to Craig Bowler who is a living expression of Christ in my life.

INTRODUCTION

What do people want more of? What is the one thing people will never turn down if you give it to them? What do people talk about the most, spend the most time pursuing, and think about most often? The answer is...money.

In 2014 a large global asset management company did an on-line survey among U.S. investors. The survey included 458 affluent investors with a minimum of $200,000 in investable assets not including their homes. The results were quite intriguing. The survey found these investors spent an average of one hour and twenty minutes each day thinking or worrying about money. That adds up to more than 9 hours each week.

The investors surveyed spent more than 20 full days a year worrying about money...and that is just on average. 10% of the investors surveyed spent 2-3 hours each day thinking about or worrying about money. That's 30-45 <u>days</u> a year. Does that give you a little context?

Granted, this was a survey of people with investable assets, people with money. Regardless of how much or how little money you have, people spend a lot of time thinking and concerning themselves with money. If you spend time thinking and worrying about one thing, you aren't spending that same time thinking or worrying about something else.

INTRODUCTION

It's tough to think and worry about money AND something else at the same time. We focus on one thing OR the other.

Money is at the root of most conversations, most of our actions, and most of our relationships. In turn, money is the goal of our businesses. It serves as the foundation of all government services and operations. Everything said and done these days leads you to believe that money is what makes war, peace, love, and the entire world go around. Maybe it does...or maybe it tries to make you think it does.

Money takes many shapes and forms in the verbal and mental conversations we have with ourselves and with others. It is too often the origin of the majority of our thoughts, words, and actions. Money is either directly or indirectly involved in most of what we say and do.

Money is evidenced in the Christmas gifts we give and when and where we eat out with friends and family. Money is a factor in the activities of our children and in the vacations we take. How we entertain ourselves, the business deals we pursue, our homes, cars, clothes, and the food we eat all speak to how much money we have and how we decide to spend it. Take money out of all of these activities and the conversation either drastically changes or doesn't exist at all. Add money to the conversation and it changes; subtract money and it changes again. The amount of money we have can help us make or lose friends, determine where we live, and direct what we do. People don't like to acknowledge that money dictates so many of the basics in our lives, but it can and usually does just that.

I have spent 30 years in the financial services industry. My job has been labeled "stockbroker," "financial consultant," and "financial advisor." Regardless of the title, I have spent almost three decades dealing with money and the people who possess it. During my career, I have learned quite a bit about the characteristics and qualities of money. I have seen it work in and shape the hearts and minds of people from all walks of life. I have seen what the lack of money as well as the abundance of money can do to people. I have seen the effects of both new money and generational money. I have seen money come and go in people's lives, fortunes made and fortunes lost. I have learned a lot about money and its relationship with people.

With all that I have seen in 30 years of working with people and their money, one thing is crystal clear to me: unless we make a direct effort to understand how ubiquitous money is in our hearts and minds, we can be ruled and mastered by it. Listen to the news, read publications, watch the actions of our governments and you will see the prevalence of money. There don't seem to be any problems that money doesn't create or can't solve: wars, famine, poverty, unemployment. According to the experts, a little more or less money and these problems could all be avoided. We are so consumed by money that we often don't even recognize its importance in our lives.

Watch your own thoughts and actions to see how integral money is to your life. Listen to what your friends talk about and observe where they spend their time. Marital satisfaction and the unity of the family can rise or fall with varying socioeconomic levels. The amount of money we have and how we use it can alter the function of the core units of our lives. Marriage for money or divorce for lack of it, money influences our homes and hearts.

More money is not always good; less can be detrimental, as well. Governments, individuals, and businesses focus on money morning, noon, and night. We debate income inequality or too much asset concentration in the hands of too few. We ponder how to get money, what to do with it, and how to manage it. Regardless of the question, money has its part in the conversation all of the time.

Money opens up opportunities and closes doors based on the amount we have or pursue. Many critical decisions are made based upon our finances. Stay-at-home mom or two-parent working family? Public or private school education? What college can we afford? Our relationships can be restricted or expanded by our socioeconomic level. Money is such a powerful force that it can cause people to see only the dollars and cents in the decision and not the real person or the morals behind those figures.

Money can be a master that makes people grapple with many questions. Some people think that money demands answers from them. How much money do they really need? Are they spending their money the way they should? How much should they give away? What does their money really mean? All along the way, people who ask these questions fall subject to money's mastery. People can become so intimately intertwined with money that they view it and themselves as one. And this view can preclude God from our thoughts and decision-making—or at least put His perspective and teachings on the back burner.

I have seen money take the headlines and make the headlines in people's lives. I have seen money make people think they are smarter and better than others because of an abundance of money. I have also seen the lack of money make people think they are less intelligent and less blessed by God than those with more money. All in all, I have seen money and the pursuit of it become front and center in the hearts of believers and non-believers alike.

This book is not meant to either demonize or glorify money. The point of these writings is simply to recognize the premise that money is so intricately tied to our hearts and minds that it is critical to seek Godly wisdom on the subject. As Christians, there is one place to start and one place to finish when seeking to understand a subject: the Bible. We must not rely on reason, logic, intelligence, or data to understand money. We have to rely on the life and teachings of Jesus.

To answer the questions we have about wealth and its uses, it is critical to look at the life of Jesus. What did Jesus say about money? What did He do with it? How did He use or not use money? What did the people closest to Jesus learn from Him about money? What did the Son of God and the Son of Man say and do to give us a better understanding of our finances? I want Jesus to speak to us through His Word and tell us what He knew to be truth.

This is not an all-encompassing tome on money. On the contrary, it is a brief look at lessons we can learn about money from the life of Jesus Christ. I encourage you to walk through some of His teachings in an attempt to recognize how money shapes your thoughts and actions. I encourage you to see where Jesus drills down in each case to a point where someone makes a choice between money OR.....their faith in Him to provide, the chance to choose between Him or their riches, the opportunity to listen to earthly wisdom on money OR what Jesus had to say. My hope and prayer is that these words will open your heart and mind to what Jesus wants to teach you so that you may understand His will for you...and your money.

ASK YOURSELF...

1. Is it possible that money or the pursuit of it, either through my job or through other activities, has taken anything away from me putting God first in all areas of my life?
2. Do I think more or less of myself or others because of the wealth or lack of wealth we possess?
3. Do I show favoritism to or judge a person or an activity to be either successful or a failure based on the monetary reward it yields?
4. Do I recognize situations that my faith dictates I choose either Jesus OR money?

If your answer is "yes" or even "maybe," then wade with me into a conversation with Jesus and the Holy Spirit regarding money in your life.

chapter 1

JUDAS'S STORY

Christ taught about money with His words, but He also taught about money with His actions. Some of His most compelling lessons involved the people closest to him—His twelve disciples. He chose twelve guys to be His disciples and share His life. Let's look at one of them: Judas.

You probably remember that Judas is the one who betrayed Jesus in the Garden of Gethsemane. Isn't it ironic that Judas was the disciple in charge of all the funds for Jesus' ministry? The one person that Christ allowed to control His ministry finances was also the one who betrayed Him. Ten of the twelve disciples abandoned Jesus, but only one betrayed Him...the guy with the money.

In trying to understand more about God's perspective on money, it's important to study the story of Judas. It is interesting to see how Judas acquired money, what he did with it, and what it did to him. We need to observe what Jesus said to Judas about money as well as how He dealt with the guy in charge of his funds.

Let's establish the fact that Jesus knew the people He was choosing to spread His message. He knew His disciples inside and out. Maybe Jesus just slipped up with Judas and put the wrong guy in charge of the finances...or maybe not. Maybe He

21

teaching us something through everything He did.

But Jesus would not entrust himself to them, for he knew all people. He did not need any testimony about mankind, for he knew what was in each person. – John 2:24–25

If Jesus knew Judas's heart and what he was capable of doing, why did He choose Judas as a disciple, much less allow him to be in charge of the finances? Was He teaching us in greater depth about money principles? Was He teaching us about our need (or lack of need) for money? Was He teaching us about what money can do to our hearts? Was He teaching us more about what can master a man and what a Master can do with a man? Was He teaching what money does to a person if that person sees it as more critical than it actually is? Was he showing us that when our faith is tested or we lose our faith in God money can be a red flag to show we have chosen between the two? Christ didn't rent out meeting places. He didn't hire caterers or plan elaborate events to "reach" people. So how important was money to Jesus?

It's sometimes tempting to cheat by going straight to the end of a story so we can get to the bottom line. That would be the wrong thing to do in this case. We don't want to merely focus on an end result in order to draw our conclusions; rather, we want to evaluate the entire journey to learn all we can. Let's dive in to discover the red flags in this story of Judas and an incomparable betrayal.

A week before The Last Supper, a dinner was given in Jesus' honor. The money guy, the man in charge of the ministry funds, took center stage. How and why did Judas get front and center of this event?

> *Six days before the Passover, Jesus came to Bethany, where Lazarus lived, whom Jesus had raised from the dead. Here a dinner was given in Jesus' honor. Martha served, while Lazarus was among those reclining at the table with him. Then Mary took about a pint of pure nard, an expensive perfume; she poured it on Jesus' feet and wiped his feet with her hair. And the house was filled with the fragrance of the perfume. – John 12:1–3*

What a setting! What a celebration! Jesus had raised His friend from the dead. The atmosphere had to have been thick with awe, relief, and outright pure joy! Everyone's thoughts must have been consumed by an outpouring of love and wonder... right?

> *But one of his disciples, Judas Iscariot, who was later to betray him, objected, "Why wasn't this perfume sold and the money given to the poor? It was worth a year's wages." – John 12:4–5.*

"I got my mind on my money and my money on my mind." So who's thinking about money right this minute? Judas, that's who. The guy with the purse strings; the money, not the talent. Jesus' brother James said that everyone should be quick to listen, slow to speak, and slow to become angry. Our words reveal our hearts, and Judas was quick to speak. His first response to Mary's worship was, "What are you doing? You're wasting valuable resources!" So where was his heart? Where was his worship?

After an initial blush at Judas's comment, his point actually doesn't sound too out of line. His question seems to be legitimate, even if his timing was bad. If you or I had seen the same extravagant display, would we have asked the same question—or at least had the same thought? Maybe we wouldn't have jumped to a conclusion as quickly as Judas, but would we have gotten there later that night or the next day?

In today's philanthropic world, there is a great deal of focus on both the effective use of donated funds and the accountability for "evidence-based results." Would you support a ministry that didn't at least ask the same question as Judas, even in hindsight? Wouldn't we expect the same question to arise at a board meeting as the board evaluated that evening's dinner? Was Mary's utilization of such a valuable commodity the highest and best use of her assets for the promotion of the ministry?

Would money concerns cause us to ask the donor why she didn't exercise a little more reason and discretion in her expenditure? The data would definitely not support her actions as wise. Could you have sat there and not judged her actions? Isn't it the job of a treasurer or a board to make such a judgment? Aren't they supposed to be the experts? If Judas had the purse strings, wouldn't he be considered the expert?

Many times, we assume that we know the best way to use money without even asking God. After all, He has given us the ability to reason deductively. Objective data would have supported a better use of Mary's expensive perfume than to lavish it on Jesus' feet. But Jesus seemed to care more about the heart behind Mary's gift than He did about the most logical use of her treasures.

Are we slaves to the sin of "fiscal logic"? Are we more concerned with the wise use of money than with the heart behind the funds? How often do you and I put dollars and cents before our hearts, as revealed to us by the Holy Spirit through prayerful discernment? When it comes to the use of money or property, how often do we ask God first, even in the most logical of cases? How often do we let money and logic serve as the master of our decisions, causing us to not even consult God? Far too often, I'm afraid.

"No one can serve two masters," Jesus said. It is either one master OR the other. John's account of Mary's profuse worship reveals that one's expressions about the importance of fiscal logic or evidence-based results may mask a darker underlying reality.

> *He did not say this because he cared about the poor but because he was a thief; as keeper of the money bag, he used to help himself to what was put into it. – John 12:6*

John gives us an even clearer picture of Judas's motives. Judas had been a thief, and everyone knew it. So everyone knew it, yet Jesus still let Judas be in charge of the ministry funds? Who was at fault here, Judas or Jesus? Isn't it Jesus' responsibility to make sure the ministry funds are accounted for? Had Jesus never heard the saying, "The buck stops here"? What does this tell us?

A more troubling question might be this: If Jesus knew Judas was a thief, not to be trusted with money, why did He put—or keep—Judas in charge of His money? Jesus may not have given Judas the job initially, but surely He could have taken it away from him. Was Jesus giving him the chance to choose?

Too often we decide that when God blesses us materially, we have a green light from Him blessing our ability to make wise decisions with it. We tend to believe that if we have more money, and if we are striving to live for Him, God has ordained us to be His stewards over much. So how are we different from Judas...or are we? How fine is the line between a thief and someone who is arrogant enough to believe he is capable of making financial decisions without continually seeking God's guidance?

Jesus let it play out with Judas for all to see. In a small group of guys, Judas's reputation wasn't much of a secret, at least among them. Among your friends, what is your reputation? We often view our material blessings as God's ordainment of our business or economic acumen. Are we like Judas and don't even know it? Is God letting a bigger picture play out in our lives like he did with Judas? Stop here and now, change your mode of operation, and get back to the basics of talking to Him about every financial decision you make for yourself or for others.

Jesus was teaching us far more than simply the relationship of money to His ministry. He was teaching us that money reveals the heart. Money can reveal issues of the heart and be a red flag to what may lie beneath the surface of your actions and words. It can prevent or be an excuse for not serving what your true master desires. When your faith is tested, watch what you do with your money. Watch your money, to see how your faith is tested. Jesus had little need for money except as a means of revealing to men how their desires for material things can prevent them from loving and serving others.

So how did Jesus respond to Judas's self-serving call for the prudent use of wealth? A year's worth of wages had been dumped on His feet. Couldn't Mary have found a better, more modest way to express her love for Christ?

> *"Leave her alone," Jesus replied. "It was intended that she should save this perfume for the day of my burial. You will always have the poor among you, but you will not always have me." – John 12:7–8*

Let that one sink in for a minute or two.

Did Jesus really just say that? Did He really mean what he said? That's not a very wise use of money; isn't wisdom with money important? Yes, but Jesus obviously values the heart more than money. The value in Mary's declaration of faith is not measured in dollars and cents. Mary's love for Jesus defied all logic, and Jesus loved her for it.

Jesus is more important than money. Period. However much you may want, need or believe money can quantify your worship or equate to your devotion, it can't. Don't judge yourself or others. Be careful putting money in the same discussion as worship.

This story has profound significance for present-day ministries. Are our concerns about fiscal logic and evidence-based results pushing us away from radical and public expressions of love for Jesus? How many donors would agree to use their money or property in such an elaborate show of love as Mary? What responsible treasurer or board member wouldn't raise the same objection as Judas?

We are supposed to be wise with the money entrusted to us. Where is the logic of dumping such an expense into an expression of worship? Where is the data to support such use of ministry funds? Where is the reason behind such an outpouring? Do logic, data, and reason sometimes expose what is most important to us? Do they often reveal our real master? Do they give us an "out" from our emotions and heart response to God's calling?

This story does tell us one thing. Each time before we use the logic, data, and reason God naturally gave us, we should ask Him what He thinks about our money and its use. He may call on us to defy the logic of this world. His answer may surprise you if you give Him the chance.

So Judas helped himself to what was put into the ministry money bag. We don't know if he lined his own pockets or just spent the money for what he deemed to be in the best interest of the ministry. There's a fine line between thievery and self-glorification. We do know that Judas was strong-willed and didn't mind speaking up to share his perspective about how monies should be used.

Does this sound like anyone you know? When we are in charge of funds, whether our own or someone else's, we can be tempted to assume that we have the right or the inside track to dictate how those funds should be used. Is there anything wrong with that?

Not necessarily. But it also doesn't mean that our view or decision-making is always right. It doesn't mean that following the prudent—or the accepted— use of money is right. Jesus works "outside the box."

If we want His will and His way in our lives, we'd better consult Him in every situation...and not act before He gives us direction.

Let's get back to the story and read Jesus' reply to Judas's outburst of worldly wisdom.

> *"Truly I tell you, wherever this gospel is preached throughout the world, what she has done will also be told, in memory of her." –*
> *Matthew 26:13*

The man with the money—the man with his hands on the purse strings—not only got shot down by the Son of God; the woman who'd been accused of having foolishly wasted a year's wages' worth of assets was praised by her Savior. Judas had the money but confused having the cash with having the wisdom to use it correctly. Maybe he was exercising earthly wisdom and not heavenly wisdom? Does that even sound remotely possible today? These days, most people assume that having the resources means you have the ability to dole them out appropriately and responsibly. Maybe Judas should have chatted with Jesus about the entire matter. Or maybe he should have just adjusted his mind, heart, and actions to what Jesus was telling him. He had a choice of listening to Jesus OR....

This is where the story starts skidding all over the place. Judas thought he had spoken wisely. So he got angry. He decided he'd had enough.

> *Then one of the Twelve—the one called Judas Iscariot—went to the chief priests and asked, "What are you willing to give me if I deliver him over to you?" – Matthew 26:14–15a*

We don't know Judas's heart and mind, but we can observe his actions and words. He had decided to betray Jesus, the Christ. Maybe his comments reveal that his heart was no longer submissive to Jesus. Judas had issues with how Christ was setting up the Kingdom of God here on earth. His words and the fact that he brought money into play are a red flag for deeper issues. The apparent straw that broke the camel's back was Judas's view that Jesus had not only accepted Mary's wastefulness but had encouraged it. Judas's love for Jesus had faded, his faith had failed. He chose to betray Jesus and allowed money to become a new master. Money now showed itself as his master and he determined to not only leave Jesus but to betray Him—and get paid in the process.

Judas threw in the towel on Jesus and His ministry. Money did not cause Judas to betray Jesus, but it revealed his heart and attitude. When he was weak and his faith was tested, money exercised mastery over his love and faith in Jesus. He revealed his heart in the process. Not only did he walk out; he sought more money—a reward from his true master—in the process. He chose something other than Jesus.

So they counted out for him thirty pieces of silver. – Matthew 26:15b

Money can do to you what it did to Judas. It can show you where your real devotion lies. Money can show your lack of submission to Christ and become a force to replace your faith and worship. After that, the manifestations can go everywhere. It can cause you to no longer "support" a friend, a missionary or a ministry because you believe they aren't handling their finances the way they should. Money can cause you not to listen to what the God of the universe is saying to you and become your new master. It can allow, give you an excuse, a reason to betray God, turn a deaf ear to Him, and want more of the one thing that is competing for your heart.

Money can lie to you without you even knowing it...at least not right away.

> When Judas, who had betrayed him, saw that Jesus was condemned, he was seized with remorse and returned the thirty pieces of silver to the chief priests and the elders. "I have sinned," he said, "for I have betrayed innocent blood." "What is that to us?" they replied. "That's your responsibility." So Judas threw the money into the temple and left. Then he went away and hanged himself. – Matthew 27:3-5

Judas's allowed money to become the master of his heart, his words, and his actions. Then money betrayed him in the same way he had betrayed Jesus...as it often can. Money can be such a controlling force that it can cause us to lose all reason and hope and to think it will never return. Judas had seen Jesus forgive sins, heal wounds, and bring the dead back to life. Was money's pull so powerful that it lured Judas into the ultimate disloyalty to Jesus, or did it just reveal a deeper issue of submission, love and self-centeredness? Money, his new master, had rendered him deaf, dumb, and blind.

chapter 1

"No one can serve two masters. Either you will hate the one and love the other, or you will be devoted to the one and despise the other. You cannot serve both God and money." – Matthew 6:24

When money becomes your master and your basis for decision-making, it can take the place of anything and everything, even if just for a while. No one is immune to the lure of money—not one of the original twelve disciples, even you or a lifelong believer. When money, not our submission to Jesus, is the main factor in deciding how and where you spend your time and resources, the road ahead can lead anywhere. And it usually does.

We have observed that Jesus teaches us about money today by letting us examine the ways He interacted with the people who shared His life on earth. We've seen one example in Judas. If others studied our lives, what would they learn from our examples? What has our past shown to be at the center of our financial decisions? What will our future decisions reveal?

With whom do we choose to spend our time? How do we act with these people in situations that require spending money, donating money, and communicating about money? And more importantly, do we make our own decisions about how to spend our resources, or do we seek God's guidance and submit to Him in "managing the moneybag?" The Word of God is a great place to learn about money. What do people learn about the use of money from us?

ASK YOURSELF...

1. Is it possible that money or the pursuit of it, either through my job or through other activities, has taken anything away from me putting God first in all areas of my life?

2. Have past monetary blessings made you forget we are stewards of money and not masters of it? Do your past financial decisions show your expertise or are they a reminder how God has led you and not always the data?

3. If we are stewards of money, do you ask the owner of the money you are responsible for, how to allocate it each and every time it is used?

4. Where have you been exercising discretion over money when you should be seeking God's guidance? Do you listen to Jesus OR money?

5. Where has logic, data or experience replaced the Holy Spirit in your financial decisions?

6. Do your decisions about money raise any red flags about your submission to the Spirit's leaning in your life? Do you rely on the Spirit or your experience or personal desires?

chapter 2

YOU GIVE THEM SOMETHING TO EAT

What did Jesus teach us about money through His words and His actions? Sometimes He directly addressed the use of money, and sometimes He spoke volumes by not even acknowledging the subject. Jesus lived out His personal views about money, the ways in which it should be spent, and if and when it should be used at all. Sometimes Jesus said it best when He said nothing at all.

At the peak of His popularity in ministry, Jesus attracted crowds. Not just small gatherings of people; not just hundreds, but thousands of people. Thousands of men, women, and children would all come together at one time to hear what the man had to say. Sometimes you hear more in a crowd than you do one on one.

In Jesus' day, people didn't advertise or have event planners for their gatherings. Jesus simply walked around town and people congregated near Him. He knew the size of His following; He could see the crowd in the morning when He woke up, and they stayed with Him all day long. The crowds were getting bigger. There was no surprise for the Son of Man.

chapter 2

The apostles gathered around Jesus and reported to him all they had done and taught. Then, because so many people were coming and going that they did not even have a chance to eat, he said to them, "Come with me by yourselves to a quiet place and get some rest." – Mark 6:30–31

This was a busy day. The disciples had returned from their missions, and Jesus knew they needed some down time, some quiet time, and a little solitude to recharge their jets. Jesus was constantly aware of all their needs and knew how to meet each one. People need food, rest, and shelter...and Jesus was attentive and timely in providing these things for those who were with Him. He does the same today.

So they went away by themselves in a boat to a solitary place. But many who saw them leaving recognized them and ran on foot from all the towns and got there ahead of them. When Jesus landed and saw a large crowd, he had compassion on them, because they were like sheep without a shepherd. So he began teaching them many things. – Mark 6:32–34

Jesus first tended to his disciples' needs. But then, as He witnessed the gathering of a much larger crowd, His first response was compassion. He was always in touch with people. He loved them; He felt responsible for them. A shepherd knows his sheep, their needs, and what is required to meet those needs. And this Shepherd did, as well.

YOU GIVE THEM SOMETHING TO EAT

By this time it was late in the day, so his disciples came to him. "This is a remote place," they said, "and it's already very late. Send the people away so that they can go to the surrounding countryside and villages and buy themselves something to eat." – Mark 6: 35–36*

How often do you say the same thing? If you're in a position of authority or responsibility and a situation like this arises, you might make a similar assessment and recommendation. Harmless, right? It was late; folks were getting hungry. It was time to eat. But what were the disciples' motives or the deciding factors behind their recommendation? Was theirs—is yours—pure and altruistic? Were someone else's best interests at the core of the disciples' words, or was there another motive, did they allow another master to dictate their recommendation? Everything seemed fine up to this point.

But he answered, "You give them something to eat." – Mark 6:37a

The disciples saw the need and deduced that the need could best be met with money. We can infer from Mark 6:35–37 that the disciples were questioning both how much would have to be spent to buy food for all the people and whether or not those resources should simply be given away. The picture is becoming clearer, and so are the hearts of the disciples. Money became a different issue when their own funds were being used. Money caused them to focus on their ability to provide and the physical things of this world at the expense of

37

looking to Jesus. They were so blinded that they didn't recognize Jesus wasn't telling them to go out and spend money. When you start thinking that money is the answer or you look to it and not listen to the voice of the Spirit it becomes difficult to see or hear anything else. Seem familiar? Sound like anyone you know? Does the shoe sort of fit? If you can answer yes to any of these, keep reading.

As soon as the disciples brought up the subject of cash, the entire day started to change. It had been a day of sharing, of spending quality time together, of harmony. Jesus didn't deny that the people were hungry; He just didn't see the need for money in order to feed them. Do you think that the man who had been taking care of people's needs all day long didn't see this one coming?

What ministry leader or ministry team would have let the day pass without at least bringing up the subject of food? Was Jesus keenly aware of everyone's needs all day long—until now? In fact, Jesus didn't seem to see the need to go anywhere to get anything. Jesus' words and actions were saying that money wasn't in the equation...but no one seemed to be listening.

How often do we respond in the same way? How often do we see a need and immediately look to money as the answer? People are hungry; let's buy some food. We want to share the gospel; let's plan an event, build another church, expand our campus by adding a bigger building, build a new facility, plan a mission trip. And, oh yeah, we can't move forward without funding these things first.

Christ didn't check the coffers before He started teaching that day. How can you minister without checking into the expenses and cash balances that might be required for that ministry? Don't we need to see what we can afford before we start? Do you support any ministries that don't do this? Is this ministry with excellence?

I'm not saying that planning ahead is wrong. In fact, planning is a natural and Biblical first step. But, don't let money be the driving force to proceed with a plan or the lack of money be the brick wall to stop you when God is at work. Listen to the Holy Spirit and His direction, not an abundance or lack of funds to determine your actions.

Jesus was more interested in seeking God's kingdom first, knowing that all the rest of the things He needed would be given to Him (Matthew 6:33). This account illustrates that Jesus was living out His understanding that if we care for people's souls first, trusting God to do His part, what we end up with may be far greater than money could have bought in the first place.

Jesus wants to teach us to be dependent on Him and not dependent on our money or a plan of action. The only way to learn dependence is to have the need for Him. The disciples were stuck out in the middle of nowhere. Jesus had everyone right where He wanted them. Are you right where He wants you or are you where you want to be?

How often do we get stuck trying to see how God is going to provide the money to meet our needs instead of simply trusting that He will meet them? *What if we get hungry? What if it gets late in the day? What if we are in a place where there is no food? What if we are in a place where we have no money? Would we allow that to happen? Not if we can plan around it!*

What if we began looking for Him to meet our needs instead of looking to money first? Has it been a long time since we've seen Him provide for our needs *without* money, perhaps because we have so much of it that we never give Him the chance to prove Himself? Has He provided for our needs without money, but we either didn't recognize that provision or didn't give Him the credit? Maybe we steal glory from Him by even placing money into the equation. According to this narrative, Jesus didn't even bring up the subject of money in His response to the disciples' remarks.

> *They said to him, "That would take more than half a year's wages! Are we to go and spend that much on bread and give it to them to eat?"*
> *– Mark 6:37b*

The disciples had been thinking about the problem. In fact, they had quantified it pretty accurately: eight months' worth of wages. Money was on their minds, but should it have been? Money would have been the logical solution to the problem. How often do we respond in the same way? We figure out the costs. We define the benefits, quantify the return, and evaluate the data.

Jesus said to "give them something to eat." How could the disciples give what they didn't have? How can I give what I don't have? Or how can I get it without having to buy it? Maybe I'm looking in the wrong place...or maybe I need to reevaluate the situation.

Let's not forget that the disciples are flat-out questioning both Jesus' answer to their question and His judgment. Should we "spend that much on bread"? If we ask Jesus what our money should be spent on, even a basic, legitimate expense, does He really know the best use of our money? Do His plans for our money meet with our approval?

The problem we have with asking Jesus how to spend our money is that we often don't really want to hear His answer. We tend to think that we know how to spend money on everyday stuff, and odds are that at some point we have actually asked Him about our spending and not really liked the answer He has given us. If He answers us the way He did the disciples in this story, I don't know if many of us would ask twice. We don't ask for the truth because we can't handle the truth. Maybe we just honestly don't like it. The question we need to ask is this: are we submissive to the truth once it is revealed? Do we have such a preconceived idea of the truth that we don't even hear Him speak to us on money matters?

> *"How many loaves do you have?" he asked. "Go and see." – Mark 6:38*

Too often, we just ask Jesus yes-or-no questions. Too often, we don't listen for His answers or recognize them when they don't come back clearly "yes" or "no." How often do you ask Jesus a question about money, and He answers you with another question? Think about that for a minute. Can you come up with a single example? Yet when we look at the letters in red, it seems like all He does is answer questions with more questions. Hmmm. <u>Are we really asking?</u> Do we really listen for His answer, or do we listen for what we want to hear?

Typically, when we come to Jesus with a question about money, it's a yes-or-no or an either/or question: Should I support this ministry?

Should I spend the kids' college funds on this school or that one? Do you really want me to just give them the money? Does that couple really need my money? Is that the ministry I should support?

We tend to look to Jesus to tell us whether or not we can spend money in a particular way. We don't necessarily ask Him how to spend it...or make it...or invest it. We often don't even ask Him if He even wants us to use it in the first place. This scriptural narrative illustrates how we tend to think money is essential to the conversation when Jesus doesn't believe it to be so.

In truth, we are no different than the disciples. They didn't ask Jesus what to do about feeding the hungry people. They didn't even ask Him if the people should be fed. They told Him what needed to be done. Was this common sense, arrogance, or weakness? Do we continue to tell Jesus how money should be used by not bringing Him into the conversation until the situation becomes too big for us to handle?

Why did Jesus wait so late in the day to acknowledge the people's need for food? In the first part of this sequence of events, Jesus immediately dealt with the disciples' needs by taking them by boat to a quiet place. The disciples were so busy they didn't even have a chance to eat. But Jesus' answer was to slow down, chill out, and just be with Him. What about the food? Maybe they ate, maybe they didn't, but Jesus tended to the need He believed to be most pressing.

At the end of the day, had Jesus become so preoccupied with teaching that He was unaware of the crowd's increasing need for food? Or was Jesus waiting to see how the disciples might try to satisfy and care for this need? Like most of us, the disciples quickly determined that the solution to the need was money.

When the disciples permitted money to enter the equation, they quickly reached their own conclusion without even asking the guy in charge. Does this sound like how we deal with Jesus regarding money? The situation needs cash, I have cash: decision made. No need to bother God with this one.

After all, God has given us common sense regarding money. Does this enable us to determine which people can take care of themselves and which people can't? Does it enable us to conclude when people can take care of themselves or not? Having money tends to make us think we can pass judgment on who can afford what, and when they can afford it. When money is our master, we make decisions for God and for other people without remembering that all people are His, and that He should always be consulted before we spend our money. We can exercise good judgment, but not until we have consulted with God...and yes, on _every_ move. We can exercise heavenly wisdom when we have decided to have faith in Him alone.

Being a steward of anything means you should have an understanding and know what the owner wants done in all matters. When we focus on being a steward of money, we must constantly stay in touch with God. His plans for, need of and use of money is not always what we can understand. He uses money to mold, teach and demonstrate about the condition of the human heart. We use money more to accomplish change in the physical world.

We have taken the concept of stewardship so far beyond what God intended that we have lost sight of what it really means. We have perverted our roles as stewards by treating money as if it were our own,

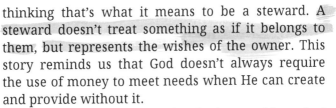

thinking that's what it means to be a steward. A steward doesn't treat something as if it belongs to them, but represents the wishes of the owner. This story reminds us that God doesn't always require the use of money to meet needs when He can create and provide without it.

The only way to know if and when and how God wants us to use money is to ask Him—ALL of the time. Sounds like doing so would be a pain—for us and for God—doesn't it? Sounds like not using the reason, logic, and data He gives us would be a waste, right? Ask the disciples what Jesus' response was to them. We confuse having money with having a green light to exercise our own judgment on its use without asking the Owner. And, we assume a lack of money means the Owner wants to go in another direction. When the money isn't there, we just need to stop and look to Jesus. We need to wait on Him to make His move.

In this story, Jesus didn't think money needed to be used to meet the need at hand. There is no way we would have reached that conclusion on our own without asking Him first. The disciples were fortunate that He was in their presence. Unless you and I stop to pray and ask Him for wisdom in spending the resources He's given us, not making our prayer a closed-ended, yes-or-no or multiple choice question, we will miss the boat entirely...and maybe miss the blessing and the miracle God wants to do in our midst. A common-sense solution to the problem in this scriptural account would have caused the disciples and all the people in the crowd to completely miss what happened next: a miracle. A common-sense solution would never have allowed the power of God to work through the disciples. And

YOU GIVE THEM SOMETHING TO EAT

often, a common-sense solution will not allow God's power to work through us.

> *"How many loaves do you have?" he asked. "Go and see." When they found out, they said, "Five —and two fish." Then Jesus directed them to have all the people sit down in groups on the green grass. So they sat down in groups of hundreds and fifties. Taking the five loaves and the two fish and looking up to heaven, he gave thanks and broke the loaves. Then he gave them to his disciples to distribute to the people. He also divided the two fish among them all. They all ate and were satisfied, and the disciples picked up twelve basketfuls of broken pieces of bread and fish. The number of the men who had eaten was five thousand. – Mark 6:38–44*

Holy mackerel! We <u>need</u> to go and tell them to take care of themselves...NOT! We need cash and a lot of it...nope, not really. We only need Jesus. When we bring money into the equation, we have a tendency to put it ahead of everything else. It can become our master. When we think money is required to fix a problem or meet a need, not only can it cloud our judgment; it too often takes center stage, removing Jesus from the picture entirely. In this case it was Jesus OR money to feed the thousands. Jesus was enough.

> *"No one can serve two masters. Either you will hate the one and love the other, or you will be devoted to the one and despise the other. You*

cannot serve both God and money." – Matthew 6:24

We can put money before God and not do it on purpose. Money is a powerful master. When we put money first, we rob both God and ourselves. We rob Him of the pleasure of providing for His children, displaying His power and receiving glory for it. We rob ourselves of the blessing of witnessing Him do miraculous works in our midst. We are ill equipped to know when money is needed to meet a need without asking Him first: every time, any time, and all the time.

It may seem like spending money requires simple reasoning or good stewardship. But if money is involved, you had better make it a spiritual issue. I'd rather see a miracle than eat dinner back in town. God would rather receive glory for His provision than to see that glory go to someone or something else. We can miss deeper spiritual lessons when we look for the quick material fix. The bottom line is that we don't want to limit God by only looking to the almighty dollar to answer questions and meet needs.

How and when God meets our needs is different than how and when we meet our own needs. When we take control, money gets a seat at the table too quickly...and it's usually at God's expense. God can meet our needs without money. And money will compete with Him and try to take credit and glory away from Him. Using money to meet all of our needs and the needs of others most often draws attention to us. Remember the original sin. Money can be a spotlight for vanity even if we're not the ones who turn it on.

YOU GIVE THEM SOMETHING TO EAT

Our God is jealous and consuming; money can be consuming, as well. Our God is full of mercy and grace; we can be the same by the power of His Spirit: money never has been and never will be. Money can try to mimic mercy and grace but it is solely dependent on the one who uses it and instructs its use.

We don't want to demonize money. Remember: God <u>can</u> be glorified through the use of money to meet needs, but only when <u>He</u> <u>directs</u> us in its use. This fine line can be confusing, so it's important that we keep a level head when dealing with financial matters. Money can be a master if the heart places it before God. We can experience an intense struggle between God and our money unless we actively put God first...in everything, all the time.

Keep a check on the level of your heart's true love for God versus the balance in your checkbook or bank accounts. Look to God for each and every one of your needs, and don't try to satisfy your own desires for anything. This sounds crazy and impossible, but so does providing dinner for fifteen to twenty thousand people with just a few loaves of bread and two fish.

So why didn't the disciples just ask Jesus what to do about feeding the crowds? Well, why don't we ask Him about how to meet our needs? Why don't we ask Him how we should proceed in helping others? Because we don't always like the answers. Because Jesus can seem scary and unpredictable. Because doing things God's way is rarely our way... and we like doing things our way.

And because doing things God's way can cost us in more ways than one. God's way can cost us money. Let's look at that next.

ASK YOURSELF...

1. Have you planned God out of areas of your life? Is there only a chance for God to direct your plans if and only after they don't succeed?

2. Have you asked God to bless your finances and financial plans without consulting Him to begin with...only in hindsight?

3. Will you stop right now and ask God to consult you about His approval for your finances and plans for your money?

4. Where can you start asking God open-ended questions about money and how you use it?

chapter 3
ROLE MODEL POSTER BOY

We can learn what Christ thinks about money by observing His interactions with people, like Judas. We see His perspective on the use of money when He tells the disciples to feed the multitudes instead of turning them away and sending them back to town. Now let's look at Jesus' words to better understand His viewpoint on money.

If we really want to know how Jesus feels about money, what He thinks about it and what He wants us to know about it, why not just ask Him? If you are looking for heavenly wisdom on anything, there is one place to start. Money reminds us there is a heavenly based wisdom and an earthly based wisdom that are at odds with each other The conflict between the two perspectives can create a trial for us regarding money and its use. James, the younger brother of Jesus, spent his life growing up with the man and spoke to this issue.

> *If any of you lacks wisdom, you should ask God, who gives generously to all without finding fault, and it will be given to you. But when you ask, you must believe and not doubt, because the one who doubts is like a wave of the sea,*

and tossed by the wind. That person should not expect to receive anything from the Lord. Such a person is double-minded and unstable in all they do. – James 1:5–8

There it is; it's pretty simple. Ask and it shall be given to you. So why didn't the disciples ask Jesus what to do on the day he turned five loaves and two fish into a feast for thousands? Why did they *tell* him what to do in a money-related situation instead of just asking Him? Why don't we ask God what He thinks and how He feels about every situation involving money?

Maybe we don't really want His wisdom with regard to money. Maybe we think that if He wants to tell us something about the subject, He'll bring it up and not wait on us to question Him. Maybe we do ask Him some things about money, but we don't hear an answer. Maybe we have asked Him in the past and heard an answer, but we didn't like the answer we heard.

If we profess to be Christians and are seeking to be more like Christ, we probably do talk about money with God. We may actually concentrate on it too much in our conversations with Him. Either we have some money and want more of it, or we want to know what to do with what we have. That's what we're supposed to do, right?

Here's a suggestion: let's get our minds off of our money. Let's quit thinking and talking about it so much...to Him and to everyone else...and make Him, and Him alone, our focus.

At the end of his account of the fish and the loaves, Mark reminds us:

ROLE MODEL POSTER BOY

...for [the disciples] had not understood about the loaves; their hearts were hardened. – Mark 6:52

The disciples lived with Jesus day in and day out. How could they not have understood about the feeding of the crowd that day? Why were their hearts hardened? James says we must believe and not doubt. Was there doubt in the disciples' minds before or after they recommended to Jesus that He send the people back into town to buy their own food? Christ told the disciples, "You give them something to eat." Did they doubt their ability to do what He told them to do?

Doubt is a natural by-product of the struggle between flesh and spirit. Trials test our faith. We look to God to gain wisdom and get His perspective on issues that cause us conflict and consternation. The resulting struggle to understand and accept His will and ways is a testing ground of submission on every issue in our lives, including money.

When doubt enters your mind, you can become double-minded, you can become unstable in all you do. Ask God where the money is going to come from to pay your mortgage. If you don't get an answer, what emotion springs up? Doubt! If His answer is to trust Him and His ability to provide for your needs... doubt springs up again. Whenever we can't see or touch or quantify the dollars to meet our needs, doubt can explode in our hearts and minds. It is in this valley of doubt we need to lean on and listen to Him more intently.

The disciples had just seen Jesus wreck a business and, potentially, the economic system of an entire community—in order to cast demons out of just one man. Jesus didn't appear to show a lot of concern for people's economic well being if their income or its source got in the way of what He wanted to do. Maybe Jesus wasn't the best person to ask what to do in situations with money. Did the disciples have the experience and data to prove that Jesus could be a wild card when it came to money? Absolutely. Could that have led them to doubt His authority when it came to the subject of money? Quite possibly.

There is a risk and a cost involved when you ask God about money. He may not answer your question right away—and timeliness may be an important factor to you. He may answer—but you may not understand what you hear. You may actually hear and understand His response—but you don't like the answer He gives. His answer may seem so far out of the realm of possibility that doubt enters your mind as to His ability to bring that answer to pass. When you ask God about money, there is always a cost. You must give up your right to use your money as you see fit and trust Him to lead you to manage your money as He desires.

Mark records the account of a guy who had a personal encounter with Jesus. This young man was seeking Godly wisdom. He wasn't coming to Jesus to ask Him about money; this fellow was asking Jesus about what mattered most to him. In fact, this guy was a role model for you and me as to how to seek Christ. He was a lot like us today: he was running after Jesus. We should follow his example in this way.

As Jesus started on his way, a man ran up to him and fell on his knees before him. "Good

ROLE MODEL POSTER BOY

teacher," he asked, "what must I do to inherit eternal life?" – Mark 10:17

What a beautiful picture! This man knew what was important and he knew where to go to get the answers to his questions. His head was on straight and his actions showed him to be a wise man. He didn't let anything stop him from running to Jesus and asking the question to which we all want an answer. He showed tremendous respect by falling on his knees before the Lord.

This man had no embarrassment, no apparent pride, and seemingly no ego. He was submissive before Jesus. Nothing got in the way of this man's pursuit of the living God. He was forsaking all others and seeking Jesus. He was giving Jesus an open-ended invitation to speak into his life and to direct his heart and his mind. Then and now, this man was a role model for following Christ.

Maybe this guy sounds like you...and maybe he doesn't. Maybe you want to seek God this way, but you don't. Then again, perhaps this man's heart sounds like yours, even if your actions don't line up. We go to God in prayer with an open heart and mind. We seek Him in private and corporate worship. We may even run to Jesus, wanting and needing an answer, just like the guy in this story. This man is our brother. He is you...he is me...he is a role model for pursuing God.

"Why do you call me good?" Jesus answered. "No one is good—except God alone. You know the commandments: 'You shall not murder, you shall not commit adultery, you shall not steal, you shall not give false testimony, you shall not

53

defraud, honor your father and mother.'" –
Mark 10:18–19

Jesus responds when we ask Him questions.
Jesus reminds us that God alone is truly good. God is
the standard. God has given us His Word to see and
know His will. His standards are written in our
hearts as Christians. You know the commandments.
Christ reminds us of His truth and confirms that
truth to us.

> *"Teacher," he declared, "all these I have kept*
> *since I was a boy." – Mark 10:20*

Thank you, Jesus. Thank you, Holy Spirit. We go
to church. We are saved. We keep these
commandments. Our hearts and minds are on track
with God's desires for us. This guy gives Jesus an
honest answer, probably similar to what we would
profess to Him ourselves.

How often do we give God the same answer as
this guy? *I'm not a murderer. I don't run around on*
my spouse or steal from others. I make a conscious
effort to never lie or defraud anyone. I honor my
parents. I'm a good person.

We may seek God earnestly and strive to follow
His commands. We want to go deeper with the Lord.
We want Him to feed us spiritual meat, to grow us to
maturity. We are after His heart.

Lord Jesus, what more must we do?

Are you the guy in this story? When you're alone
with God, is this the cry of your heart? When you get
still and quiet, when you and Jesus get one on one,
when you feel like you're really talking with Him

and are really in sync with Him, hearing His voice—is this your response to Him?

So now there's a two-way conversation going on with Jesus. Your heart and mind are wide open. You've sought Him, found Him, and asked Him. What more does He have to say?

Are you still pursuing Christ after such a confirmation, or was that enough for your quiet time today? Did you get a good word from Him and head off to work or to bed? Did you hear what you wanted and needed to hear? Too often, we get a good word and then get back to our own agenda without going deeper with God, asking Him to take us to another level of relationship with Him. You've got to want to know God more deeply; you've got to be willing to risk your own agenda and reputation. What can happen if you do? Stay with the story.

The guy in our story wanted more. He stuck around to hear what Jesus had to say next. Again, he is a role model for seeking the Lord. Are you willing to be a role model for Christ? It will require stepping out of the box you've been in and, most likely, letting God out of the box you have put Him in.

> *Jesus looked at him and loved him. "One thing you lack," he said. "Go, sell everything you have and give to the poor, and you will have treasure in heaven. Then come, follow me." – Mark 10:21*

Before revealing a word Jesus said, Mark reminds us that Jesus looked at the man and loved him. When we approach God as openly and honestly as this man approached Him, He sees us. Jesus looks at us and knows who and what we are, and he *loves* us. First and foremost, before He replies and teaches us, He loves us. What He says next He says in love.

We should never experience any fear or hesitation in approaching God about anything. This story shows us that we can approach Him openly and speak our minds. When we do, He knows exactly how to answer our questions. He gets right to the heart of the issue...and He loves us.

Jesus was honest. He didn't sugarcoat His response to this earnest man. The tough part about Jesus' words is that they go straight to the bigger issue: eternal life. Everything else pales in comparison to where we will spend eternity. And Christ can tell us exactly how to spend eternity with Him. If we really want the truth, we have to make sure we can handle it.

Our problem is that we've all sought God's answers to our important questions at one time or another and gotten the same feedback about our heart's condition. If we put anything in our hearts ahead of God OR in place of Him, He will bring it front and center. The toughest thing for most Christians to admit or realize is that money can occupy their hearts the same way as it occupies the heart of the man in this story.

Maybe you ask God about everything except your money. Maybe you don't want to stoop so low and ask God about such simple or earthly things. Maybe these earthly issues need to be addressed. Maybe your money and your stuff is the real conversation you need to be having with Jesus.

This guy is a poster child for too many Christians. We talk about salvation and eternal life. We seek guidance from God's Word. We run to Bible studies, small groups, or one more mass. We allocate quiet time to talk to God about what is pressing on our hearts and minds. We have the best intentions, but our hearts are at war. We can be knowingly or unknowingly sharing space on the throne of our hearts with God and money. We can be trying to serve two masters.

If we are brutally honest and open to hearing what God has to say about the condition of our hearts, we might—God forbid—hear the same message that this man heard. We must at least have the courage to ask God to reveal the true nature of our hearts, and then we must decide whether or not to respond to this revelation and realign our lives with His Word. Give God the chance to speak to you. Give God the chance to save you.

God wants to have an open, ongoing dialogue with us about everything. However, money's role in our life is frequently a stumbling block...and we don't even recognize it. God wants to first expose our hearts and then transform them. He has answers to all of our questions, but we can be so scared, so full of doubt about what He might say to us, that we become double-minded in all we do. Maybe we have become so self-centered and don't allow Him to speak into deep places that we haven't been in a long time.

Do you have the guts to ask Him what you need to do to inherit eternal life? This guy was willing to go deeper with Christ, but are we? Are we possibly so beholden to money as our master that this story frightens us as it pertains to the condition of our hearts? This story can be mistaken to be one in which Jesus is teaching against money. On the contrary; He is not teaching that money is evil, but instead is cautioning us against allowing money to fill our hearts so completely that there is little to no room left for God. We *know* that money can play too much of a role in our everyday lives. We *know* it can occupy our hearts to some degree. We *are* the man in this story.

> *At this the man's face fell. He went away sad, because he had great wealth.* – Mark 10:22

If the God who loves you tells you what is best for you, and you cannot or will not obey Him, there is reason for sadness. This man had the most honest response I can imagine. He heard Jesus' words and recognized truth when he heard it. We do, too. But when we hear the truth, do we respond in obedience? Do we go away sad? Or do we just go away? And where do we go after that? That's a tough question with a potentially scary answer. Either way, it is very costly.

The guy in this story is the role model and poster boy for Christians. So often, money is the stumbling block in our relationship with God and we never even know it. For far too many people, it may be the stumbling block to their eternal salvation. If this is the condition of our hearts, don't we need to know about it? Don't we <u>want</u> to know? If money is a stumbling block in our lives, we don't have to choose it over God and walk away sadly. Stay with the story.

We need to come to terms with the condition of our hearts and have faith in a God that heals, forgives, and restores. Pride and vanity may be our core problem, but only God can reveal that. Jesus tells this guy to sell everything he has, give the proceeds to the poor, and to follow Him. When Jesus talks about money, it is always related to the state of our hearts. In this case Jesus made it clear, the choice was faith in the Father OR his stuff, his money.

Christ saw a poor widow put two small copper coins worth only a fraction of a penny into the collection plate at the temple. He saw others throwing in large amounts of money. His words rang clear.

> *Calling his disciples to him, Jesus said, "Truly I tell you, this poor widow has put more into the treasury than all the others. They all gave out of their wealth; but she, out of her poverty, put in everything—all she had to live on." – Mark 12:43-44*

The problem most people have with Jesus' teachings about money is that they think He wants us to give it all up...or at least to give until it hurts. God is the Master Gardner. It's not His desire to hurt you, but He does specialize in pruning. If your heart has another master, another god you've placed before Him, pain may unfortunately be the byproduct of that false god's removal. If so, the short-term pain of extracting that idol will be worth enduring for the long-term gain of knowing Jesus and living only for Him. Do you believe this? Are you willing to find out?

God wants to get us in shape for eternity, not for the beach. God is more interested in you being in shape for the race of life, the long run, the marathon of all your years on earth. If money is weighing down your heart and mind, He may need to cut it out of your diet completely. Cold turkey. And that is what scares us the most. Why? Because we love us some money.

Jesus can provide everything you need. The disciples may not have always understood this concept, but they saw it in action when the Lord fed the multitudes with next to nothing. The key for us to live in this truth is to allow Him to do the providing. Instead of looking to your money to provide and care for you, give God the chance to meet your needs.

> *Jesus looked around and said to his disciples, "How hard it is for the rich to enter the kingdom of God!" – Mark 10:23*

Jesus said it out loud. He didn't throw it on the table for discussion; He stated it as a fact.

Clearly understand what He said. Listen to His words when He speaks. Let this statement sink in deeply. Don't kid yourself about who He's talking about, either. He's talking to you and me.

Don't listen to Satan when he tells you to turn and walk away upon hearing these words. The devil twisted God's words in the Garden of Eden; don't let him do it here. Jesus is not against wealth. Jesus is simply saying that it's hard for people who are consumed by wealth to get into heaven. Are we consumed by wealth and don't even know it? There is only one way to find out.

So how do you handle money correctly? Ask Him. Listen to everything He says, regardless of how crazy it may sound. And don't doubt. Respond in obedience.

Jesus' reply to the rich man in this passage reveals that even when we don't think an issue is about money, it often is. We may be choosing our money over God and not know it until we go much deeper with Him. The weight of money can drag down our hearts so much that it steals our affection for God and places our eternal life in jeopardy. We tend to think that our money is just a tool we can use when it actually uses us instead.

> *The disciples were amazed at his words. But Jesus said again, "Children, how hard it is to enter the kingdom of God! It is easier for a camel to go through the eye of a needle than for someone who is rich to enter the kingdom of God." – Mark 10:24–25*

The more money you have, the less you may realize that it controls and masters you. The less money you have, the more aware you may be of the struggle between the two. Either way, it doesn't change the fact that money can keep us from obtaining eternal life. Money battles with God Himself to be the master of your heart.

When Jesus specifically addressed the subject of money, His words were direct and sharp. Let's review a passage we read in our last chapter:

> *"No one can serve two masters. Either you will hate the one and love the other, or you will be devoted to the one and despise the other. You cannot serve both God and money." – Matthew 6:24*

Listen to His words. Let them soak in. We can serve only one master, never two. Our Savior drew a direct correlation between our relationship to money and our relationship to God. Nothing else wars to be your master—not your family, not your job, not your hobbies—the way that money does.

You may recognize the battle, or you may be like the guy in our story, never realizing your struggle until you give God the chance to speak into your life. We all have to choose between God and money and it's not a one-time decision. Sadly, it's a decision we have to make regularly. And when we do, we mustn't doubt what He says; we mustn't walk away sadly or let our hearts harden.

> *The disciples were even more amazed, and said to each other, "Who then can be saved?"* – *Mark 10:26*

Through Judas' example, Jesus taught that money will become the master of your heart if you allow it. You see the consequences it can wreak. Money can cause you to betray everything and everyone. It can ruin your worship; it can ruin your relationships. It can ruin your life but it doesn't have to if we let Jesus speak to us about it and then act on what He says.

Through the account of the disciples trying to determine how to feed the multitudes, we learn that money can master our minds. The disciples saw no other answer to the need to feed the thousands. They were walking by sight, not by faith. When we think that money is the only answer, we can miss being part of God's plan to glorify Himself. We can miss the opportunity to allow Him to use us, to work through us.

Jesus' words now clearly point out that money can be a stumbling block to salvation. When money becomes so deeply rooted in our hearts that we choose to trust in it instead of what Christ did for us, it calls our salvation into question. Jesus warns us that money is a master not to be reckoned with.

But this story is not over. The disciples were "amazed." Some of us are depressed right now. Others are starting to lose hope. Who then can be saved?

> *Jesus looked at them and said, "With man this is impossible, but not with God; all things are possible with God." Then Peter spoke up, "We have left everything to follow you!" – Mark 10:27–28*

Amen, Peter! We have sought Jesus; we have followed Him. As we see it, we have either left everything already, or that's what we're going to have to do. Is this the cost required for our salvation? If so, how are we supposed to live here on Earth with nothing left?

> *"Truly I tell you," Jesus replied, "no one who has left home or brothers or sisters or mother or father or children or fields for me and the gospel will fail to receive a hundred times as much in this present age: homes, brothers, sisters, mothers, children and fields—along with persecutions—and in the age to come, eternal life." – Mark 10:29–30*

Okay, so following Jesus will garner me exponential blessings. I'll get back one hundred times my investment for my sacrifice. Now you're talking to me. Poster Boy should have stuck around for this. And you and I should stick around, too.

chapter 3

For starters, never leave a conversation with Jesus early. Keep pursuing Him; keep listening to Him. Even when you don't hear what you want to hear, even when what you hear is full of pain and heartache, <u>stay with Jesus</u>. The young guy in this story walked away too soon. He obviously pitched his tent with his wealth and his "stuff." When Jesus told him to sell it all, Poster Boy was out of there. Not going back to that Bible study again. Not going to listen to that priest again. That was just a crazy thought, not the Holy Spirit.

Jesus speaks the truth, then He explains the truth. Peter pushes Him even farther...and Jesus issues a promise. Jesus' promises may not be what you want to hear, but His words are truth—you can bank on them.

We tend to want short-term gains and quick fixes in our lives. Investing for the long haul seems to be a dying concept—or maybe it's just a concept for rich folks. In this story we learn that the young man was actually investing in his money and not in his relationship with God. If his money only gave him a great life here on Earth but cost him his eternal life, how worthwhile was his investment? The young man might have been sad about Jesus' answer to his question, but he wasn't willing to do anything about it. He decided that the cost of following Jesus was, for him, too high.

Do you and I make the same decisions?

> *"But many who are first will be last, and the last first." – Mark 10:31*

There's the rub. The last thing that Jesus says on this subject is the real meat, the crux of the matter.

The last thing someone says is always the point to remember. The last thing Jesus says is the reason most Christians never finish reading this story. Are you willing to go *down* the ladder? Are you willing to risk being "last" here on earth?

The Christian who sacrifices that which is most important to his heart for the sake of putting God first will be greatly rewarded, both now and in eternity. But there is one small catch. The top dog here may be on the bottom rung on the other side of this life if he has any master other than God. The man with great wealth doesn't want to hear this because it speaks directly to him. The guy with very little wealth has just as much reason to be concerned.

It's not the dollar sum in your bank account that Jesus is concerned with; it's your heart. When He does speak directly to us regarding money, He speaks to people of all socioeconomic classes. Money can be a trap to master your heart and mind. Don't talk to God about money; talk to Him about your heart. Confess anything that you have allowed to have control over your heart aside from Him. Then listen and DO what He says.

We tend to want to figure out our financial situations on our own and not ask God His thoughts concerning our money and "stuff." We tend to rely on reason and the gifts He has given us to order our financial steps. Don't do it. Data can lie and common sense can fail us. Only God can deal with what is in our hearts. You don't know what is really in your heart unless you give Him free reign to tell you.

Poster Boy gave Jesus free reign to tell him what was in his heart. In this way, I challenge you to make him your role model. But then we learn that "he went away sad." Don't follow Poster Boy in this regard. Yield control of your heart and mind to Jesus. Be willing to sacrifice everything you have for the ultimate reward you will receive in eternity.

ASK YOURSELF...

1. When was the last conversation I had with God about my money and finances and asked <u>Him</u> to show me their place in my heart?
2. Is your financial plan and asset allocation too heavily weighted to your stuff on earth at the expense of a long term plan in eternity? How can I know without asking God?
3. Has your heart been compromised and will you let God show you if it has?
4. Am I willing to admit my heart may have been compromised by my wealth or my pursuit of money? Am I willing to find out what damage has been done over years of possibly becoming too much a friend of the world?

chapter 4
RETIREMENT PLANNING

As we study Jesus' teachings about money, we notice that He has an interesting tendency. When people come to Jesus to ask Him about financial issues, He tends to answer by not addressing the topic directly. He usually answers a question by asking another question and redirecting the conversation.

Jesus' thoughts about money can be ascertained by focusing on what's really behind the question. In His answers to the questions His followers (and His opponents) asked, Jesus pierces deeper into the asker's heart and attitudes about God. Jesus is more concerned with greater issues, like where our faith and trust lie. Jesus is concerned about issues that aren't limited by dollars and cents. We should know this as we head into a conversation with the King of the universe.

The Old Testament prophet Isaiah reminds us about the nature and attributes of God:

> *"For my thoughts are not your thoughts, neither are your ways my ways," declares the Lord. "As the heavens are higher than the earth, so are my ways higher than your ways*

and my thoughts than your thoughts." – Isaiah 55:8–9

Americans seem to have an abundance of both money and questions about money. A large quantity of anything naturally turns our attention and focus to that very thing. By definition, abundance means excess. Abundance is more than we need. No matter the quantity, we are responsible for what we have been given.

> *"From everyone who has been given much, much will be demanded; and from the one who has been entrusted with much, much more will be asked." – Luke 12:48*

Without guidance from the Holy Spirit, our natural thought processes cannot always be trusted. Data can't always be trusted, either. Isaiah reminds us that God's way of thinking is not our way. God's ways are higher than ours; His thoughts are higher than ours. Through His provision with the fish and the loaves, the disciples learned that God's ways were not their own. Judas learned the difference between his way of thinking and Jesus' way of thinking when he expressed his opinion about Mary's lavish outpouring of expensive perfume on her Lord. The rich man learned the difference in his way of thinking and Jesus' when Jesus Himself revealed it to him.

It can be too easy to pass off the examples we have read thus far as being outdated Bible stories or just plain "old school." The abundance in which our American society lives today almost prohibits a fish-and-loaves miracle. Our ministries are incredibly well funded. Our leaders wouldn't dare set out on a mission without the proper financial support.

The abundance of our assets is overwhelming and can cause us to seek money for ministry at the expense of the leading of the Holy Spirit. The abundance of money combined with our proclivity for planning, which is good and Godly, can supersede or overpower the still small voice of the Holy Spirit. The age old dilemma is alive and on steroids today. We must be careful not to buy into the same trap the disciples did thousands of years ago. Too often we seek money before we seek Jesus.

Money has become so deeply rooted and prioritized in the hearts of believers that a modern-day Judas would probably never be part of a ministry like Jesus'. We have too great a regard for money and too much reason, common sense, and data to support a Jesus-type ministry in the 21st century.

What about the young man who turned away from Christ because he was told to sell everything and become destitute to follow Him? Too many Christians have already determined that God has gifted them to make money to support the church or other needy groups. Too many believers have convinced themselves that their wealth is God's blessing, that they can handle it. These believers may miss hearing God's voice if He says anything to the contrary.

Truly, He blesses us to be a blessing to others, but the blessing of money can be so powerful and cause us to focus on ourselves and the blessing, not the blessor. If God has blessed us with money, over time, it can become our master and be powerful enough to make us forget why we were given the blessing in the beginning. This is why it is so important to <u>always</u> ask God before we spend a dime.

We're unlikely to recognize that we are like Judas or the young man in our previous story. Maybe we're not so different from the people who lived two thousand years ago. Maybe everything old is new again. Jesus spoke in parables to His "unbelieving and perverse generation" because they couldn't understand the true meaning of His words. In our modern age, we might say they couldn't handle His words. They couldn't handle the truth. Can we? Maybe a parable will work for us today, as well.

> *Someone in the crowd said to him, "Teacher, tell my brother to divide the inheritance with me." – Luke 12:13*

This sounds as modern-day as you can get. There was obviously an abundance of "stuff" bequeathed to this guy and his brother as an inheritance. Today, the offices of financial planners, estate planning attorneys, and investment advisors are full of folks like this. Can you relate? Have you been down this path yourself? Do you live on this path?

> *Jesus replied, "Man, who appointed me a judge or an arbiter between you?" Then he said to them, "Watch out! Be on your guard against all kinds of greed; life does not consist in an abundance of possessions." – Luke 12:14–15*

Inherent in this man's question was his greed for his possessions. *I want my fair share. I deserve my fair share. My fair share is my right.* Is this true for you and me? We say that we want what is right and fair, but our focus seems to honestly be on what we want... and we can want what we don't have. In the Parable of the Rich Fool, Jesus reminds us that our lives are not measured by our possessions.

Jesus continues to teach us about His heart toward money and possessions:

> *And he told them this parable: "The ground of a certain rich man yielded an abundant harvest. He thought to himself, 'What shall I do? I have no place to store my crops.' Then he said, 'This is what I'll do. I will tear down my barns and build bigger ones, and there I will store my surplus grain. And I'll say to myself, "You have plenty of grain laid up for many years. Take life easy; eat, drink and be merry."'" – Luke 12:16–19*

This is the American dream! This is the free enterprise system at work. It's what you work for every day. This story explains how God blesses a man's labor. It sounds like the story of a modern-day American Christian. You can relate to this guy; this man is either you or someone you know.

The man whose fields produced the good crop is the featured speaker at a men's ministry event you have attended. Successful Christian businessmen are heralded and sought after for their wisdom and business acumen. Our perception of this parable is that common sense and smart planning yield God's blessing. But once again, Jesus is more concerned about our hearts than He is our worldly success.

chapter 4

This parable is an example of retirement planning at work. The man needs bigger barns to store what the land and the Lord have provided him. Your growing business may need a larger warehouse to distribute your product. You may need additional locations for your successfully growing franchise. You may need a bigger home for your growing family. The man in the parable was going to be wise with the fruits of his labor. He could see retirement looming before him. He could see the prospect of more time to spend with the kids and the grandkids.

But God's ways are not our ways. His thoughts are not our thoughts. What did Jesus want to teach us through this parable? What does Jesus have to say about our wisdom in such matters?

What does Jesus have to add to this retirement-planning scenario?

> *"But God said to him, 'You fool! This very night your life will be demanded from you. Then who will get what you have prepared for yourself?' This is how it will be with whoever stores up things for themselves but is not rich toward God." – Luke 12:20–21*

The man in this parable didn't stop to ask God what to do with his new blessing; he just asked himself! He had been successful in the past; he knew what to with an abundant crop. Maybe you've experienced the same thing. One blessing follows another and, therefore, you should repeat the process, right? This blessing follows the previous one, so why do I need to ask God for direction again? I know how to prosper, and I know how to plan wisely. A good crop is a green light from God, so full steam ahead! Store it up before it goes to waste.

Planning for retirement is smart and wise. Planning for life before death at the expense of life after death is wrong. The man in this story was thinking of himself first, not others. God wants us to put others before ourselves. God wants us to put Him before ourselves. Jesus gives us "a new command" to remind us that we should not make ourselves the focus of attention.

> *"A new command I give you: Love one another. As I have loved you, so you must love one another. By this everyone will know that you are my disciples, if you love one another."* – John 13:34–35

How much is enough to set aside for retirement? The rich man in this parable already owned fields and barns. How much is enough? How often do we fall prey to the same temptations as the guy in this story? When do we cross the line and put money first in our planning, forgetting to ask God His priorities? Jesus told the man in this story to stop serving himself and start serving God.

Money is not bad, but wealth is deceptive. The more money we have, the greater the risk can be that we will be deceived and allow money to become our master. That's a tough pill to swallow for the prosperity-minded American Christian. The successful Christian businessman doesn't speak to the deception his wealth carries with it, but he should. The keynote conference speaker speaks to the fruit of his faith, philanthropy and giving, not the worries and deceitful nature of wealth. He speaks to what money is, how he uses it wisely and how it is a good thing. Maybe he even speaks to how money is not true wealth.

Jesus reminds us of this in the Parable of the Sower:

> *"The seed falling among the thorns refers to someone who hears the word, but the worries of this life and the deceitfulness of wealth choke the word, making it unfruitful." Matthew 13:22*

When we attend a conference or hear a successful Christian businessman, the allure and deceitfulness of wealth can target our hearts and minds. This deceitfulness can suggest to us that a good life and faith in God results in the reward of money. It is easy to be lured into the pursuit of <u>more</u> money because we equate it to God's blessing. We can be fooled into pursuing <u>more</u> money on an equal footing with pursuing God when the two are presumed to be so closely tied together. This is a trap in modern day American Christianity. Faith and monetary success are not interchangeable and not directly related.

Television shows, magazines, news networks, and entire industries are built around both our hunger to have enough and suggestions about what to do with the abundance with which we are blessed. People flock to seminars and spend countless hours planning in order to "have enough." It all amounts to having *more*. It all centers on *self*.

Jesus speaks directly to our obsession with ourselves. We put ourselves ahead of others, and we put ourselves ahead of God. When we don't stop to ask God what to do before taking a single step each time we receive a blessing, we fall prey to the deceitfulness of wealth and the potential trap of the love of money. And we don't have to acknowledge that we love something to actually love it.

The Parable of the Rich Fool shows how easy it is to seat ourselves on the throne of our lives. Having an abundance of money can just reinforce that position. Our preoccupation with money and its management is not the problem, but the symptom. Our real problem is neglecting to serve our True Master. The problem is having another god before the One True God. The problem is that our personal desires can betrayed the Savior of our Souls.

Money can take center stage so quickly. What do *I* do with money? How do *I* handle money?

God has blessed *me* so greatly with this abundance of wealth. God has given *me* the talent of making money. God has given me the responsibility. Once we take the focus off of God, placing it on our money or ourselves, it can become very tough to remember that it's not all about us.

We know that for every one of us, life's going to end with us finding ourselves six feet under. Life after death begins with our last breath. Jesus called the man who focused his planning on himself a *fool*. We must remember not to concentrate so much on our worldly future at the expense of using the blessings God gives us to care for other people today.

How many generations does your estate planning cover? How much of an inheritance do you plan on leaving your kids and grandkids? How much do you need for retirement before you consider what others are living without today? To know the answer you have to listen! The question isn't whether to store up more or not. The question is whether to listen to God OR... Don't store up money for yourself without being rich toward God. Don't be a fool! (Jesus said it, not me.)

This parable transcends time. Jesus spoke in parables more than two thousand years ago, not only for His generation but for our generation today. This parable should stick in our minds and weigh heavily on our hearts. This parable is about having faith in yourself OR God. This parable should haunt us every morning and every night until we allow God to help us determine what—or Who—is the master of our hearts.

If you're the successful businessman to whom all the young guys look or the one that the older guys study to "learn how to be successful," meditate on this parable before you offer counsel again. Don't present a message just in secular terms, where it can shine a light on your own wisdom and intelligence. Don't forget the risks, deceitfulness and potential downsides of wealth in your next speech. Jesus tells us be rich toward God. Share His perspective on success and wealth with others. Let your message— and your example—shine the glory on God.

We think we know when enough is enough, but we don't. As long as our focus remains on our own views about our money without asking God first, we will never get it right. This parable should stop us dead in our tracks! Stop concentrating on building your business, and start investing in your eternity. Stop thinking that you have all the answers, and start seeking God for His answers. The guy in this story waited too long. Have you made the same mistake?

It bears repeating: God's ways are not our ways. Our ways are earthbound, short-term, and selfish. God's ways are higher and so are His thoughts. Consult with God before you make another decision regarding your business or your money. Your very life may be required before the day ends. Consider the risk that Jesus is declaring in this parable. Trust in Him and not in the size of your retirement account.

ASK YOURSELF...

1. When and where have I failed to consult God before I consult my own financial plan?
2. Where have my successes made me focus on what I want to do with monetary rewards before asking God what He wants?
3. Am I putting my faith in God to tell me when to sell my business, when to build it, when to store up my treasures OR am I trusting myself?
4. Am I listening to God as much today as when I started my plans for retirement OR have I tuned Him out and don't hear Him anymore?
5. What is the risk to my life and finances if I don't ask and hear the voice of God in my financial planning?

chapter 5
THE DISCIPLES
NARROW THE FOCUS

You and I are so much like the disciples who walked with Jesus two thousand years ago. When we study His teachings regarding money and wealth, we find that we're in a similar predicament to that of the disciples. They heard Jesus' words but often didn't understand them. They were confused. Even the Lord's parables left them scratching their heads.

When Jesus left this world, the Father sent the Holy Spirit to live in us and to guide and teach us. It was through the Holy Spirit that the disciples shared the life and message of Jesus Christ with the world. The Holy Spirit worked through the disciples to share Jesus' teachings and perspective on money and wealth with others.

Sometimes it's easier for a man to understand another man. The disciples and apostles spoke clearly about the meaning of Jesus' teachings on the subject of money and wealth. Their words are very pointed and direct. They are such an encouragement to modern-day believers! The disciples did not speak in parables but instead went straight to the bottom line in real-world terms.

Let's focus on the disciples' instruction concerning money and wealth as they learned about the subject from Jesus. They focused on the big picture—the substance of His message—without quoting Him directly. These guys stuck to the core of Jesus' teachings while challenging us to seriously consider and apply His message.

God's Word speaks to us when we are tempted to only exercise human reason and common sense regarding things of this world. Paul reminds us that applying reason and data without the confirmation of the Holy Spirit can serve to build up yourself instead of the Kingdom. Paul spoke directly to those who think and act solely according to facts and figures.

> *"Do not deceive yourselves. If any of you think you are wise by the standards of this age, you should become 'fools' so that you may become wise. For the wisdom of this world is foolishness in God's sight. As it is written: 'He catches the wise in their craftiness'; and again, 'The Lord knows that the thoughts of the wise are futile.'" – 1 Corinthians 3:18–20*

So how do we proceed? How do we know what God wants us to do with our money? How do we know when enough is enough to provide for our retirement? Paul declares that our own wisdom can be foolishness in the sight of God. How can we take another step forward in the conversation about wealth when we know it can be such a slippery slope toward greed and the love of money?

Our best option is to realize that human wisdom must be replaced by God's wisdom—His point of view. As believers, we have the Holy Spirit as our Counselor. We must elect to heed the counsel that is *not* of this world before listening to the counsel that is. Prayer is the only place to start.

> *For the foolishness of God is wiser than human wisdom, and the weakness of God is stronger than human strength. – 1 Corinthians 1:25*

No money to feed thousands of people? No problem for Jesus. You call an extravagant worship experience to the tune of a year's worth of wages wasteful? He calls it beautiful. You say it's unnecessary to go to the extreme of selling everything you own to free your heart from another master? Jesus says that because you love your stuff so much, you need to sell it to be free. God says that when I put myself before others by building more barns to store up my blessings, I am being a shortsighted fool. When we get ahead of God and start rationalizing our actions ahead of heeding the promptings of His Spirit, we are in danger. Regardless of how many causes you may be able to fund for the church, if God hasn't directed you to do it, don't.

God wants us to run from anything and everything that can come before Him. Wealth is deceptive. How do we determine that we have "enough?" We can be too earthbound to even recognize when we cross over the line from using money to loving it. No financial planner can tell you where that line is. No advisor can know your heart. We can be so deceived by this world that we don't even know ourselves. No reason or data can tell us what's in our hearts. There's nothing in this world that can give us the wisdom we need. Only God can do it.

But God chose the foolish things of the world to shame the wise; God chose the weak things of the world to shame the strong. God chose the lowly things of this world and the despised things—and the things that are not—to nullify the things that are, so that no one may boast before him. – 1 Corinthians 1:27–29

Think about these words the next time you seek counsel in order to make a decision. If you request the advice of a "high-profile professional" before you seek Godly counsel, let that be a red flag. If you solicit advice strictly from "successful" people, think again. Ask God where to go for advice. His answer may surprise you.

When we study Jesus' teachings about money, they can be just as confounding to us today as they were to His disciples. Jesus' direct words regarding wealth can be haunting. Jesus' parables about planning and providing can scare and confuse us. Jesus did not teach the wisdom of this world; in fact, He often spoke directly against it.

As Christ was teaching His followers that it is impossible to serve two masters, the Pharisees were listening in. Jesus took His message to them a step further and made His point in spades.

The Pharisees, who loved money, heard all this and were sneering at Jesus. He said to them, "You are the ones who justify yourselves in the eyes of others, but God knows your hearts. What people value highly is detestable in God's sight." – Luke 16:14–15

THE DISCIPLES NARROW THE FOCUS

Once again, we must search for the application for our lives. Man's ways are not God's ways. What man finds highly valuable, God detests. So whom do you trust? Whom do you believe? Do your actions line up with Jesus' words?

The disciples knew Jesus' thoughts about money because He constantly conveyed and embodied them. Jesus' words are not suggestions. Jesus' words are truth; they are fact. They are the first and last data we need to consult and consider in our decision-making. They are the only "reason" we need to exercise.

Jesus cares about our souls; we tend to care more about our stuff. Jesus can judge our hearts; we can't even judge our own, much less someone else's.

When the disciples taught others about money and wealth, they narrowed it down to the big picture: they taught Jesus and Him alone.

John was the disciple whom Jesus loved. John was one of the first disciples called by Christ and the last of them to die. John was the disciple that Jesus asked to care for His mother, as if she were his own, as He hung dying on the cross. John stayed with Jesus from His ministry through His trials to His death on the cross, and he showed up three days later at His grave. John knew Jesus intimately. He studied Jesus.

When John wrote his letter near the end of his life to encourage Christians in their faith and to remind believers not to stray from the original teachings of Christ, he addressed the struggles and dangers of money and the things of this world.

Do not love the world or anything in the world. If anyone loves the world, love for the Father is not in them. For everything in the world—the lust of the flesh, the lust of the eyes, and the pride of life—comes not from the Father but from the world. – 1 John 2:15–16

"Do not love the world or anything in the world." These words are not really hard to understand; these words are hard to handle. Nothing is more representative of the world than money. From a worldly perspective, money makes the world go 'round.

James was Jesus' brother. He grew up with Jesus. James was a leader in the church. He was actually skeptical about his brother's Lordship until he saw Him again after His crucifixion. After seeing the risen Christ, James got busy. If anyone could speak directly to what Jesus thought and taught, James was well qualified.

You adulterous people, don't you know that friendship with the world means enmity against God? Therefore, anyone who chooses to be a friend of the world becomes an enemy of God. – James 4:4

A friend of the world is an enemy of God. This statement is clear. James directs his proclamation to "you adulterous people," not to "anyone who is sold out to the world." He says that those who are "friends with the world" become God's enemies, not those who are "haters of God." The difference is subtle. James knew that the allure of being a friend to the world can easily lead to the love of that world—without most people even recognizing the process—so he chose his words carefully.

THE DISCIPLES NARROW THE FOCUS

James was speaking about the world "system" that battles against the heavenly "system." Jesus wanted us to love people and not judge the unbelievers. But James knew that the ways of the world were diametrically opposed to the ways of God. James emphasized recognizing and knowing the difference between being a friend to people in the world and being a friend of the world's systems.

James frankly states that the love of this world and the things in it is hatred towards God. How easy it is for us to find ourselves in this perilous state! Jesus' words about our inability to serve two masters come rushing back. He said there are two masters, God and money, and that we cannot serve them both. Period.

We serve our masters. We tend to emulate our gods. Jesus has stated that we are incapable of recognizing who and what we serve without His input. If you have yet to ask God to reveal the areas of your life in which you are not putting Him first, you need to. If you have asked Him, ask Him again. Judas was so consumed by the god of money that he didn't get the message before it was too late. Avoid that possibility at all costs.

While you're at it, ask a brother in Christ (or two) who—or what—they see you prioritizing and worshiping. A Christian brother can sometimes see your heart better than you can see it yourself. Try to not only ask people who benefit monetarily from their relationship with you for their input. This may be hard to do. It may exclude your pastor or your best friend. How many relationships do you have with people from whom you don't seek financial gain or to whom you don't provide financial support? Evaluate your relationships to determine the role money plays in your interactions. This

chapter 5

exercise serves as a reminder that money is so intricately woven into the fabric of our lives that it is hard to remain objective about it. Money is so firmly positioned in our lives that it is imperative for us to keep it under God's direction.

John directly warned us about money. James threw the subject in our face. And Paul penned a very pointed reminder in his letter to Timothy:

> *For the love of money is a root of all kinds of evil. Some people, eager for money, have wandered from the faith and pierced themselves with many griefs. – 1 Timothy 6:10*

The dangers that accompany money can start with eagerness. Eagerness can lead to love and, pretty soon, we are dragged away toward the full-grown love of money—and with it, sin. Our love for money can be hidden behind lies we tell ourselves. We desire money but hide it behind lofty goals. Without God's direction, we can hide the pursuit of money behind noble goals.

Some people are "eager for money." They may not be *lovers* of money; they may just be *eager for* money. We may think we are eager to give more money to the church. Eager to better care for our families with more money. Eager to do good, but eager for money in order to do it. Without God's direction, this is misguided. Paul declares that being eager for money can cause people to wander from the faith. Paul reminds us that this wandering may not lead to death, but it can lead to many griefs.

The writer of Hebrews reminds us in his closing remarks.

THE DISCIPLES NARROW THE FOCUS

Keep your lives free from the love of money and be content with what you have, because God has said, "Never will I leave you; never will I forsake you." – Hebrews 13:5

Be content with what you have. In His parable, Jesus chastised a man for building more barns to hold his "stuff"—because the man was not content what he had. His ability to have more and to get more led him to be discontent in his current situation and to put himself before others.

How do we develop the mindset necessary to live a life free from the love of money and a preoccupation with wealth? Paul tells us that we mustn't allow ourselves to be molded by this world. Paul instructs us to "renew" our minds, to have new approaches and new ways of thinking by aligning ourselves with His Word. How can we do this? Renewing our minds starts with seeking God's guidance for every decision and steering away from the love of money.

The apostles consistently warn us of the dangers of the love of money. Paul put it bluntly:

> *Do not conform to the pattern of this world, but be transformed by the renewing of your mind. – Romans 12:2*

We have a responsibility as believers to be a living sacrifice for our God and Master. We are living testimonies to the greatness of God. Whether we serve the One True God or other gods will be evidenced by how we think about money, what we do with it, and what it does with us.

How can we put the disciples' teachings into practice? To start, we need a deeper prayer life. We need to not only allow but to invite accountability partners to speak into our lives on a regular basis. We need support and input from people who aren't tied to us for material gain or employment. We need to be courageous enough to ask ourselves, our friends, and our God to show us the areas of our lives in which we are needing, wanting, and loving the world.

The ways of this world battle directly against heaven. If we do not keep our money and the pursuit of wealth in check by having a healthy individual and corporate prayer life, money can become powerful enough to turn us away from having a heavenly perspective. To escape the conformity of this world, we need to be cautious about patterns that tie our friendships to our businesses or our monetary supporters. We need to realize that God has not forsaken us simply because we find ourselves in need, and we need to recognize that we are not holy just because we find ourselves in positions of financial stability or growth.

We live in the world...but loving it can be fatal.

ASK YOURSELF...

1. Do I hide my eagerness for money behind more noble goals or ambitions?
2. Is my desire to "get ahead" a smokescreen for the love of money?
3. Am I content with what I have, or am I always striving for more?
4. Does my "stuff" reveal a love for things of this world over things in the heavenly realm?

chapter 6
IN IT, NOT OF IT

We've examined Jesus' perspective on money by observing His teachings, His actions in circumstances where money was required or involved, and the behavior of people with whom He chose to share His life, along with the consequences of their choices. Next, we focused on Christ's specific words regarding money and wealth and on the parables He told to help us better understand the topic. Lastly, we listened as the disciples narrowed it all down for us, helping us to comprehend the big picture as we study money and wealth. We learn many lessons about money through the life and teachings of Jesus, but one irrefutable conclusion we can reach is this: Jesus doesn't view money the same way most of us do.

Jesus isn't affected by money the way we are affected by it. Jesus doesn't need money or want it the way we need and pursue it. So how should we view money? And why do we have to get His input on all of our financial decisions and not simply trust our own reasoning or data as we decide how to spend our earnings?

The simplest, most obvious explanation is that Jesus was not of this world—and by natural birth, we are. Our nature stirs us to embrace the power to control, to depend upon our ability to reason, and to follow our desire to do what we want without being told otherwise. In the accounts we have read thus far, following this nature has resulted in God's people robbing Him of His glory and robbing themselves of the ultimate blessing that could have been theirs. This nature can cause us to choose between God OR things of this world. We see where men can miss the mark, even when they have the best intentions, because of the powerful hold that money has on their hearts and minds. No one is exempt from this temptation.

Jesus did nothing by accident and everything by design. In John 8, Jesus has chosen a great place and time to speak to a crowd of people about the differences between Him and everyone else on the planet. In a place where their minds were probably thinking of finances, He rebuked the Pharisees for having an earthly point of view on life and faith.

> *He spoke these words while teaching in the temple courts near the place where the offerings were put. Yet no one seized him, because his hour had not yet come.* – John 8:20

The setting was perfect, and the message was plain and simple. Jesus was reminding His followers (and His adversaries) why He thought and acted as He did. It was a great opportunity for Him to point out the differences between the Son of Man and mankind itself.

> *But he continued, "You are from below; I am from above. You are of this world; I am not of this world."* – John 8:23

IN IT, NOT OF IT

Jesus didn't pursue money or even think about it the way we do. Instead, Jesus spent a lot of time telling us to put God before anything else in our lives and to turn from the ways of this world. Jesus consistently urged us to see our lives from an eternal perspective instead of from a worldly viewpoint.

Like the folks that Jesus taught, we, too, often manage our money with worldly wisdom. What makes us think we are more capable of keeping our hearts and minds focused on God than men were thousands of years ago? What makes us think we are so much wiser today? Listen to Jesus:

> *"For the pagans run after all these things, and your heavenly Father knows that you need them. But seek first his kingdom and his righteousness, and all these things will be given to you as well." – Matthew 6:32–33*

Money itself is neither good nor bad, it can be either. It's how we approach money, how we prioritize it, and how we use it that makes it one or the other. Jesus knows that we need money to live. What Jesus did was to use the topic of money to address the condition of our hearts. He used it to prove to us how easily the things of this world can exercise tremendous power and control over our hearts and minds. He used it to show the difference between being *in* this world and being *of* this world.

Jesus' teachings about money remind us that it is sometimes easier to love something we can see and touch than it is to love something we can't. It's easier to love something that provides us an immediate, tangible benefit than something that is intangible—

at least for today. Jesus prompts us to recognize that our thoughts, our priorities, and even our faith are often shaped more by what we can see than by what we believe about God.

People are looking for God. We are searching for Him everywhere, consciously and unconsciously. It is easy to understand why we look for Him through money and with money. But, money has limits, God doesn't. Money is limited because it is of this world. It is limited by what it can do, it is limited in its amount. Money can also limit our faith. Money can divert our faith from what God can do (feed thousands on a few fish and loaves) when we look at it and not Him. The stories of Jesus remind us that He doesn't need it and too often it takes the focus away from Him.

The power of God is limitless. Christ shows us where the limits of money can take our faith and focus off of Him and constrain them both. When we limit our faith, we limit our God. When we limit God, we limit what He will do.

And he did not do many miracles there because of their lack of faith. – Matthew 13:58

When our faith and focus is limited to this world and things of this world, our blessings are limited as well. There is a story in the old testament of a widow whose husband had died and the creditors were coming to take her two sons as slaves for payment. The woman had no money, no assets, only a little oil left. God instructed her to collect empty jars and pour the remaining oil into the jars and keep pouring. When the jars were full she asked her sons for another jar. When there was not another jar left to pour the oil into, the oil stopped. The blessing was limited to her faith and action in the number of jars she had collected.

Things of this world can limit our focus, our faith and God's power. Money can limit God's power. Be careful looking for a limitless God in the limits of your money or someone else's.

Jesus knew that we would struggle to live out the lessons He taught in His time here on earth. So out of love and concern for His disciples, He modeled His teachings for us. And He prayed for His disciples. You and I are His disciples. Prior to His arrest, Jesus spoke aloud to His Father in a request for Him to protect us in the battle between worldly and heavenly things.

> *"I am coming to you now, but I say these things while I am still in the world, so that they may have the full measure of my joy within them. I have given them your word and the world has hated them, for they are not of the world any more than I am of the world. My prayer is not that you take them out of the world but that you protect them from the evil one. They are not of the world, even as I am not of it." – John 17:13–16*

As Christ followers, we are not of this world. We will always be engaged in a battle between the things of this world and those that are not; it is a battle that will only be ultimately won when Christ comes back to rule and reign on Earth. Jesus didn't ask the Father to take us out of the battle; He asked the Father to protect us in it. Jesus specifically asked the Father to protect us from the evil one.

chapter 6

There is nothing that is more "of this world" than money. And there is nothing that is less "of this world" than Jesus Christ and His followers. This is one reason why believers experience so much struggle and consternation regarding money. Whether we live month-to-month, are able to meet our needs comfortably, or have great wealth, no one is exempt from the temptation to place our trust and faith in money instead of in God Himself.

We know that what Jesus taught is the truth. We are forced to choose between the things of this world and the things of God's eternal world every minute of every day. We must recognize that money will always be a conduit the enemy can use to lure us away from God. Jesus knows we need money, and wealth can be useful under God's leadership. But Jesus wants us to use money appropriately and not let it get the best of us. Money is center stage in the battle for our hearts. Jesus doesn't want us out of the battle; He wants to protect us in it.

In Satan, we face an adversary that wields the power to tempt us with worldly desires...and he is very good at his job. The devil even tempted Jesus Christ. Why should we expect to be immune to those temptations? The devil has temporarily been given claim to all the kingdoms of the world, and their splendor is his to give away.

> *Again, the devil took him to a very high mountain and showed him all the kingdoms of the world and their splendor. "All this I will give you," he said, "if you will bow down and worship me." Jesus said to him, "Away from me, Satan! For it is written: 'Worship the Lord*

your God, and serve him only.'" – Matthew 4:8–10

This passage serves to remind us of the danger in assuming that all our material blessings come from heaven. Yes, God can bestow material blessings. But wealth may also come, in part or in full, from hell itself. Ask yourself if you have ever succumbed to temptations that have led to the acquisition of earthly treasures. If so, repent, and be reminded once again to ask God what He wants you to do with the money and possessions you have.

Jesus' face-off with Satan reminds us of the power of the allure of this world and the temptation it presents to worship things instead of God. Christ's words remind us that whatever or whomever we worship, that is what or whom we will also serve. There is no way we can overcome this temptation without seeking God first in every decision we make; there is no way to lose when we do seek Him first.

In it, we win. *Of* it, we lose.

ASK YOURSELF...

1. Have I mistaken any monetary blessing as being from God, when it may have been from Satan instead?

chapter 7
WHAT DOES MONEY HAVE TO SAY?

We've looked at what Jesus taught about money, and we've considered the examples of some of the people He spoke with about money. We've evaluated what the disciples had to say about money. Now, let's look at money itself for a minute. What are the characteristics and qualities of money? What does it do for and to us? What does money have to say for itself?

One of the biggest reasons that people, Christians included, struggle with understanding the subject of money is that money speaks to them. People write books about what having money says and means, both to and about them. People want to know what their money means.

The old adage that "money talks" is quite true. People say that money demands attention; they say money demands answers. The wealthy, along with their advisors and philanthropists, devote countless hours and a profusion of words attempting to determine money's message: how to spend it, how to save it, how to share it. Those in debt with barely a penny to their names still listen to money's voice, attempting to allocate what few funds they have to the areas that money screams it is needed most.

chapter 7

Before going any further, stop for one minute and ask a simple question. Isn't it strange that money talks? Money not only talks; it has a loud voice. Money asks us questions and seems to put answers in our mouths. Money tries to dictate and control the conversation. It's about the strangest thing since the talking snake in the Garden of Eden.

In the Garden, the snake had a voice, and Adam and Eve listened to what it said. The snake lied and deceived its way into the hearts and minds of God's people. Just like Adam and Eve should have done with the snake, we must train ourselves not to listen to money, but to listen instead to the voice of God. We must listen to Him first and not forget what He says.

Jesus said that money and God are two masters that vie for our servitude. No wonder money is so powerful! You can see money, touch it, and use it. No one has ever seen God or touched Him. You definitely cannot use God. A master directs the one who is subservient, not the other way around. If money is a master, a lot of the questions it asks probably center around how that master relates to our hearts. We must be careful to understand what money is really asking and demanding of us.

God doesn't just ask us questions; He issues commands. He commands our love and our loyalty. The top ten list of His commands starts with putting and keeping Him in the top spot ahead of everything else.

"You shall have no other gods before me. You shall not make for yourself an image in the form of anything in heaven above or on the

earth beneath or in the waters below." –
Exodus 20:3–4

As compared to Old Testament times, our gods
and idols today can be tougher to identify as such
because they fall outside the confines of religion and
its practices. In ancient times, men would make a
golden calf or other image to represent a religious
deity and then worship that image. These days, the
dollar sign is emblazoned in our minds via TV
screens, books and magazines, and just about
everything in our culture. Everything is measured
by how much it costs, and before we see the benefit
of an object, we see its dollar sign. Has the almighty
dollar become an idol and a god in our everyday
lives?

A business proudly frames its first dollar of
profit. A tombstone emblazoned with a dollar
amount from a public offering is memorialized in
office suites. A gold watch represents a successful
partnership or consummated deal. We wear and
display representations of wealth to signify what we
have accomplished. These representations can
remind us of accumulated wealth, the time we've
spent pursuing money or how we have been
rewarded for our efforts with money. Have we
made it an idol? You tell me.

Since we can see and touch money, it can be
altered and changed. Another characteristic of
money is that it grows old and can be physically
destroyed, at least for now. The world is in a race to
go cashless and ease us of this burden, but in the
meantime, we store up the physical certificates.

chapter 7

"Do not lay up for yourselves treasures on earth, where moth and rust destroy and where thieves break in and steal; but lay up for yourselves treasures in heaven, where neither moth nor rust destroys and where thieves do not break in and steal. For where your treasure is, there your heart will be also." – Matthew 6:19–21 (NKJV)

Dollar bills, rubles, yuan—all paper. Paper is nothing more than a representation of worldly wealth and value, representations of worldly riches and prosperity that can and will pass away. Along with moths and rust, inflation, deflation, and stagflation are descriptions of forces that can destroy the value of a worldly treasure known as currency. How do you secure the value of money and keep it from being exhausted? How do you make it grow? Should you? Can you?

"Do not be afraid, little flock, for your Father has been pleased to give you the kingdom. Sell your possessions and give to the poor. Provide purses for yourselves that will not wear out, a treasure in heaven that will never fail, where no thief comes near and no moth destroys." – Luke 12:32–33

I guess there are no monetary forces at work in heaven either. Oh, yeah: you can't even take it with you. Jesus said to sell it, give it to the poor, and therefore secure the value of your treasures in eternity. No more worries about having to make it grow or about it giving out on you.

WHAT DOES MONEY HAVE TO SAY?

We have to work to earn money here on earth when the Father has already given us a kingdom in heaven. Granted, this is all a result of man listening to the voice of that snake and being deceived by its words. Investments go up and down; they increase and decrease in value and, often, simply run out. A treasure in heaven can never be exhausted, and a thief can't even come near it. A treasure in heaven never fluctuates in value, and it certainly never goes away.

Money is definitely of this world, and that's okay. In our hearts, we just need to separate that which is here and now from that which is eternal. This can be tough when the thing that longs to be our master is something we can see and touch, as opposed to the One True Master, who is, for now, unseen. For the time being, money is still physical. This leads many people to believe it's a tool we can freely use. Christians are eager to use all their tools, talents, and gifts for the Kingdom. The key is to use that tool under God's guidance and not let the tool use us.

Money *is* a tool that God may choose to use to teach us His ways and to mold and shape us. But remember, Jesus never referred to money as a tool. Jesus said that money is a master that we serve, not one that serves us. For a tool to be used for the master's benefit and renown, it must be in the hands of a servant. A servant must constantly ask his master for instructions. A servant does not know his master's business. Money can deceive even well-intentioned people if they do not consistently seek His direction for its use first.

"You are my friends if you do what I command. I no longer call you servants, because a servant does not know his master's business. Instead, I have called you friends, for everything that I learned from my Father I have made known to you." – John 15:14–15

We go from servant to friend only after we have learned what Jesus' business is all about. He came to seek and to save those that are lost, and in so doing destroy the work of the devil. Jesus' business is love, forgiveness, and healing. Spend time learning everything the Father made known to Jesus. Strive to be a good servant first and foremost. Then you can be a good friend.

If God is using money to teach and mold you more into His image, don't mistake more or less of it as being a reward or punishment for what you have done. Most often, God is using the lack or abundance of money to reveal your heart and to shape your character more than to reward your behavior. That's where we can really misunderstand what God is doing and saying through money. Make sure you ask yourself if there is a conflict between what money is saying OR what the Holy Spirit is saying to you.

Jesus' brother, James, reminds us that the blessing isn't always with the biggest bank account or the most assets.

The brother in humble circumstances ought to take pride in his high position. But the one who is rich should take pride in his low position, because he will pass away like a wild flower. – James1:9-10

WHAT DOES MONEY HAVE TO SAY?

Money says the man who has more wealth is the most blessed. Money says you can look and see God's favor. When Jesus spoke He said your money has no bearing on your true blessing and position in His kingdom.

Another characteristic of money is its ability to make people and things bigger and stronger, at least from a worldly perspective. Money can build a material fortress in homes, property, buildings, businesses, and possessions. But do we use money to build up the Kingdom of God *before* we build our own kingdoms? Don't allow money to make you feel, think, or act like you are stronger just because of its abundance in your life. In turn, don't let the lack of money make you think God is punishing you. Your strength comes from the Lord, not your possessions.

Remember the landowner who had a bumper crop and responded by immediately building more barns to store his grain—before asking God what to do with the blessing? Jesus called him a fool and told him his life would be required of him that very night. We should use money to build up the Kingdom of God before storing up more and more for ourselves to become stronger in the eyes of this world. Keep in mind that even the wisest man can't define his own needs without going to God for insight first.

James, the brother of Jesus, made it pretty plain. Listen carefully to his instruction and warnings.

> *Now listen, you who say, "Today or tomorrow we will go to this or that city, spend a year there, carry on business and make money." Why, you do not even know what will happen tomorrow. What is your life? You are a mist*

that appears for a little while and then vanishes. Instead, you ought to say, "If it is the Lord's will, we will live and do this or that." As it is, you boast in your arrogant schemes. All such boasting is evil. If anyone, then, knows the good they ought to do and doesn't do it, it is sin for them. – James 4:13–17

There it is once again. We brag and boast when we don't ask God first before moving forward with "arrogant schemes." Establishing business plans to make more money without first seeking the Lord's will can be evil. "All such boasting is evil." And now that you know what you ought to do, if you do otherwise, it's sin. I didn't say it; James did.

When money talks, it can tell us many things. Although we have already established that having an abundance of money is not necessarily proof of God's blessing, money can often try to tell us how wise or foolish we are in decision-making. Money can also reinforce the lie that we are in control of our own destiny and that our decisions are the reason for our blessings. Pretty soon, we can begin to believe in our own wisdom and ability to make decisions regarding money, if not pretty much everything else. Ask Judas. Ask the landowner. Ask Jesus.

Money can also lie to us when we lack enough of it. We can hear, "You're a failure," "God does not love you," or at least, "God is punishing you." And there's always, "You lack business acumen because you haven't been rewarded with money—and that's the measure of your wisdom and worth." All lies.

The deception of wealth lies in its ability to make you believe your actions are good or bad depending on the trail of money that follows. Money can deceive you into thinking you are smart or dumb. Money can deceive you into making decisions based on the potential monetary outcome and not on God's will. Profit is not always the evidence of God's blessing, nor is poverty always His curse or condemnation. We must quit thinking in such worldly terms but instead go into every situation seeking God's guidance and direction.

Money can be used to accomplish great things for God's Kingdom...but so can poverty. Our own strength isn't always needed, called for, or desired by God. The Kingdom of Heaven actually belongs to the poor in spirit. God uses the weak, the poor, and the unwise of this world more readily than He does the rich and famous. He used a lack of provision to provide the banquet of fish and loaves in the desert. Sometimes He purposely uses less to prove that He is more—and to convict those who believe otherwise. Or, as the Bible puts it, to shame them.

But God chose the foolish things of the world to shame the wise; God chose the weak things of the world to shame the strong. – 1 Corinthians 1:27

Since money can be used to build the Kingdom of God, some people like to think of it as a means to an end. It absolutely can be, but whose end are we talking about? Faithful people are more often than not the means to God's end. In Jesus' stories, money seemed more likely to get in the way of developing people's faith in Him than it served as a conduit to greater faith. In the wilderness, offering Jesus the wealth and splendor of all the earthly kingdoms was actually Satan's means to an end. Sometimes it's better to skip the wealth to make sure your blessing comes from the right place and will serve God's desired end.

So money talks, but we shouldn't always listen to it. By listening to money before listening to the truth of God, we frequently misunderstand the meaning behind what money is actually saying. Money is physical. It is of this world and is therefore wasting away before our very eyes. Because of its physicality, it can very quickly become an idol. Money can increase and decrease; money can make men stronger and weaker. In our flesh, we tend to choose strength over weakness. Therein lies a slippery slope. Money can also been seen and utilized as a tool, but a tool is only as useful as the man who uses it. Make sure your faith is in God's ability to direct you and not in your own ability to make and multiply money.

Money can be a means to an end, but that end is dependent upon the qualities and characteristics we attribute to money. The end God desires for us is to be more reliant on Him and to be more faithful to obey His voice and commands. As long as your money directs you to know, trust, and rely on Him more, God can bless you and the money He has allowed you to steward. Make sure your money brings you closer to Christ and closer to the image of Jesus. Does your money make others see Christ more, or you?

Judas thought he was a steward in control of his money, when that money was actually in control of him. Don't let "your" money tell you the same lies. Christ didn't stop Judas from sinning, but instead allowed him to be directed by his own heart and mind. Make sure your heart and mind are always focused and faithful to your true Master and God.

ASK YOURSELF...

1. Where and when do I make plans for my business and my money without first asking God what His will is for them?
2. Have I become judgmental of others and show favoritism because they are successful from a monetary standpoint?
3. Do I let anticipated profit or loss dictate my actions before asking God what I should do in regards to my job and investments?
4. Does money speak louder to me than the Holy Spirit? How can I change that?
5. Does my money point others more to Jesus than me...how?

CONCLUSION

So what lessons have we learned about money from the life of Christ? Have you been trusting Jesus and Him alone, OR is your faith and trust elsewhere? And what do we do with what we've discovered?

CONCLUSION #1: LISTEN TO GOD BEFORE YOU LISTEN TO MONEY.

Jesus' analysis from 20,000 feet is that He is far more concerned with our hearts than He is with our money. We have got to lose all the worldly adages and earthly ways of thinking about money to understand God's viewpoint on the topic. With every decision, seek Him. Don't just do what worked in the past, He may have different plans today...ask Him.

CONCLUSION #2: MONEY IS NOT NECESSARILY THE GREEN LIGHT OR THE MICROPHONE.

Don't assume that because you have either wealth or the responsibility for it, an opinion, and no one to stand in your way, you are the expert. God is pleased when you put Him first and to do that requires constant submission to the leading of the Holy Spirit.

CONCLUSION #3: TRUST GOD, NOT THE DATA.

Don't mistake experience or cost benefit analysis for the voice of the Holy Spirit. Judas did just that, and we see where it got him. If the disciples had gotten their way in the desert, there would have been no miraculous feeding of thousands through the distribution of only a few loaves of bread and some fish. Get your mind off your money, and don't let money dictate your actions before you consult God.

CONCLUSION #4: GOD CAN AND WILL PROVIDE WITH OR WITHOUT MONEY.

He may use money as an answer...but He may not. Try asking Him first. Don't assume you rightly know when—or how much—money is required to meet needs. Don't think your judgment regarding where and how to spend money is always right just because you have the money to spend, either.

Don't tell Jesus what is needed; don't box him into a time frame. Be patient. He knows what time it is. Let Him dictate the time and place...let Him dictate the provision and how it is to be made...let Him get all the glory! Don't steal any of it for yourself. And, yes, He can still perform miracles today if we don't allow our money or ourselves to get in the way. Don't let money rob Him of glory or prevent you from seeing a miracle take place.

CONCLUSION #5: THERE IS ONLY ONE MASTER OF YOUR HEART.

At the very least, follow the example set by the rich young man, and ask the Lord what to do. Just remember to be conscious of your response after He speaks to you. Look in the mirror and make sure that the money in your possession hasn't turned you into a self-absorbed guy doing things your own way. Don't buy into the belief that God that will bless your actions because He has blessed you with money. When money becomes plentiful, it's hard to recognize when your own heart is turning away from God. In this guy's case, he didn't even see it in hindsight. Like Jesus said, it's hard for the wealthy to get into heaven.

CONCLUSION #6: DON'T FALL IN LOVE WITH MONEY OR THE THINGS OF THIS WORLD.

The disciples heard what the Master had to say about money, about what it can do to a man, about the price of answering to money instead of to God. More often than not, they didn't understand Jesus' words at the time He spoke to them, but they eventually got the message: the love of money is the root of all kinds of evil. Don't think you can master money or that it's a tool for you to use at your discretion. Money can make you the tool, and you and I are not wise enough most of the time to even be aware of that change of position before it's too late.

Where does this leave you? I can't tell you the position that money occupies in your heart. Neither can you without first asking God to reveal it to you. Then you must listen for His answer. He can and will answer. If you'll quit placing money first and focus on God instead, He will teach you everything He wants you to know.

The lessons we can learn about money from the life of Jesus begin with a few questions. Do you want to grow closer to Christ regardless of the price you may have to pay? Do you want to experience spiritual growth and take your walk of faith to another level? If you do, then engaging in a discussion about the lessons you've learned about money from Christ is a great place to start.

Does money exert more control over you than God? Do you spend more time thinking about money, its pursuit, its uses, and activities that revolve around the use of money than you do thinking about the Creator of the universe? If you did an actual analysis of your conversations and activities, would you conclude that they revolve more around money more than they do around God? Do your actions reflect your heart? Only God can tell you.

Sin takes many shapes and forms, but a common characteristic of all sin is that it leads us to want less of God and act or think as if we need God less than we do. Sin is anything that separates and comes between God and us. Sin is anything that takes the place of God in our lives. Nothing stunts spiritual growth more than sin. Does your use of money stunt your spiritual growth, or does it encourage it?

Do you listen to God more or less because of money? Does money help or hinder your relationship and dependence on God? The writer of Hebrews made it simple for us.

Therefore, since we are surrounded by such a great cloud of witnesses, let us throw off everything that hinders and the sin that so easily entangles. And let us run with perseverance the race marked out for us... – Hebrews 12:1

There are a few realities for us to learn about money from the life of Jesus.

1. GOD WANTS TO BE THE MASTER OF OUR HEARTS AND EVERYDAY LIVES.

Money battles with God to master us. More money? The greater the battle between God and money. Less money? The greater the battle between the two. You see, it's not the amount of money we have that means anything; it's money itself that causes the battle.

> *"No one can serve two masters. Either you will hate the one and love the other, or you will be devoted to the one and despise the other. You cannot serve both God and money." –* Matthew 6:24

2. GOD WANTS US TO HAVE FAITH IN HIM AND HIM ALONE.

Money can limit our faith. Whether money limits our faith by giving us the ability to supply our own needs instead of depending upon God to do so, as in the case of the feeding of thousands of people with a few fish and loaves of bread, or by providing for our future through a large retirement account, don't let money limit your relationship with God. God's power is unlimited, but our trust and faith in Him can be restricted by money. He responds according to our faith, not according to our bank statement.

> *And he did not do many miracles there because of their lack of faith. – Matthew 13:58*

God uses people of great faith more than He does people of great wealth. If we put our faith in money instead of in God, we limit His activity in our midst and rob ourselves of the blessing of seeing Him work miracles.

3. GOD WANTS TO RECEIVE ALL OF THE GLORY IN AND THROUGH OUR LIVES.

Money seeks to share or steal that glory from God. Judas acknowledged money's desire for recognition by prioritizing the value of perfume over the value of the worship of God. Jesus told the rich man to choose between his stuff and his salvation. The man with the bountiful harvest decided to tear down his barns and build new ones to hold his overabundance of grain before he even conversed with God, according to Jesus' parable.

Money can be a thief. It can lead us to try to determine the "proper" use of worship funds or to buy supper for a bunch of people instead of looking to God to miraculously provide it. In your world, the examples may or may not be obvious. The disciples teach us that our hearts can be hijacked without our knowledge. The Psalmist knew it as well, and he recommended that we have the following conversation with the Lord.

> *Search me, God, and know my heart; test me and know my anxious thoughts. See if there is any offensive way in me, and lead me in the way everlasting. – Psalm 139:23–24*

The bottom line is this: we must ask God to reveal the areas of our lives in which we've allowed money and sin to get in the way of our relationship with Him, and we must rely on His power to show us. Then we must repent. We are too often wrapped up in our own ways and in our own stuff to know our own hearts. We are lost unless He shows up and shows us the way.

4. MONEY CAN STEAL OUR HEARTS AND, THEREFORE, OUR LOVE.

We are commanded to love the Lord our God with all our hearts, minds, and souls. If money is a master, and we are certain to love one master and despise any other, money will surely rob God of our love for Him. A master commands. Who is your master?

God is jealous for our love. The church in Ephesus was tried and found guilty.

> *"Yet I hold this against you: You have forsaken the love you had at first." – Revelation 2:4*

Money can cause you to forsake Christ. Ask Judas. Ask the rich man. Ask Jesus. Have you forsaken your first love for the security, power, and safety you believe money will provide? Ask God. He is the only one that knows the answer to this question.

Make the psalmist's prayer your prayer every morning of every day of your life. Trust that He who began this good work of salvation in you will see it through to completion. You're not in this alone. Have faith in Jesus and in nothing else. If it is even possible that you have put your faith in anything other than God, stop and drop to your knees this very minute. Ask God to show you, to forgive you, and to help you before another day passes.

Ask God to teach you about money. What and when He teaches you about money through the life of Jesus is between you and the God of all creation. Whatever He whispers to you in that still, small voice, I pray you are obedient.

God, forgive us for putting anything before You. God, bless us in all the ways that You desire.

To God be the glory.

ABOUT THE AUTHOR

Parks has worked with clients, volunteers, and employees in boardrooms and corporate & private office settings for more than 30 years in regards to investing time, money and talents. He has been a financial advisor for 30 years, a husband for 32 and a father of two for more than 22 years. He is a coach, teacher, student, and servant dedicated to seeking and submitting his life to Jesus.

Made in the USA
Lexington, KY
19 March 2016